Falkirk and District Royal Infirmary

A Triumph of Co-operation

Falkirk and District Royal Infirmary

A Triumph of Co-operation

Ian Scott

NHS FORTH VALLEY

Falkirk and District Royal Infirmary
A Triumph of Co-operation
published in 2011 by

NHS Forth Valley
Carseview House
Castle Business Park
Stirling

in association with

Falkirk Local History Society

ISBN 978 0 9560480 3 5

NHS Forth Valley is extremely grateful for the financial
assistance from the Friends of Falkirk and District Royal Infirmary
to make the production of this commemorative book possible.
If you wish to support or join the Friends Trustees you can
contact them at: The Friends of Forth Valley Royal Hospital,
Chairman Bob Ness on 01324 821099.

Cover Design by James Hutcheson

Printed in Scotland by Bell and Bain Limited, Glasgow

Contents

A companion volume to this book, *Stirling Royal Infirmary: a History* by Craig Mair, is being published at the same time price £9.99. It is available from NHS Forth Valley, Falkirk Local History Society (01324 627692), the Stirling Smith Art Gallery and Museum and bookshops.

Preface

As a Falkirk 'bairn' born and bred, Falkirk and District Royal Infirmary has been part of my life since childhood. In 1989 I had the pleasure of writing a short history of the Infirmary to mark its centenary. Now, with the magnificent Forth Valley Royal Hospital open for business, it seemed an appropriate moment to look back again at the fantastic story which began with Mrs Gibson's little Cottage Hospital in Thornhill Road, continued with the much loved 1932 Infirmary at Gartcows and has reached fulfillment this year on the RSNH site in Larbert. I have chosen as the sub-title of the book 'A Triumph of Co-operation' partly because it was a phrase used by Prince George at the opening ceremony in 1932 but also because it sums up perfectly what happened in the years leading up to 1889, 1932 and 2011. On each occasion hundreds, maybe thousands of people, worked tirelessly to bring their vision to reality and in the process a bond between the public and their infirmary was formed. Today we can look back with pride at the determined efforts of the Victorian ladies and gentlemen, the incredible fund-raising activities of the 1920s and the huge logistical, financial, clinical and managerial collaboration which has given our town and district the finest hospital facilites in the land. This story is dedicated to those people of all trades and professions who for over 120 years have followed the example of the Good Samaritan and placed the health and well-being of others before their own.

Ian Scott
Falkirk
September 2011

Photographs

Most of the photographs in this book come from the archives of NHS Forth Valley and the collection of Falkirk Local History Society. Falkirk Archives in Callendar House provided two images and the *Falkirk Herald* allowed the use of several pictures from past editions, and especially the modern pictures on page 160 and 172. The photographs of the old Thornhill Road Infirmary and several others are included with the permission of Clare and Werner Gauster of the Hatherley, Arnothill.

Acknowledgements

Many people have helped me to tell this story and I am grateful to them all. Back in 1989 I thanked former Matron Miss Agnes Cadger, Sister Lucy Balmer, Mrs Jessie Cruikshanks, Sister Elizabeth Bremner, Sister Elizabeth Shanks and Miss Susan Baird and, sadly, several of them are no longer with us. Thankfully Miss Cadger is still to the fore and I would like to take this chance to thank her once again and wish her well for the future.

The late Andrew Tomney allowed me to use extracts from his own reminiscences back then and I have once again found them extremely useful in recounting the FDRI story in the post war period. This time I had a great deal of help from Jessie McGregor, Lena Sutherland and Margaret Tomney who gave up a lot of their time to help me with their memories and I thank them very much indeed. Tom Whyte was a fund of information and helped locate a great many documents and photographs without which the book would have been much the poorer. Others within NHS Forth Valley like Alexis Archibald, Margaret Ogston and Communications Manager Kate Fawcett were always ready to clear the way for me to access records in the health archives and I thank them for all their support throughout this project. I am grateful too to the Chairman and Secretary of the Friends of Falkirk and District Royal Infirmary, Sandra Peat and Bob Ness, for their assistance and for helping to fund the publication.

Clare Gauster from Hatherley, the great granddaughter of the celebrated Mrs Gibson, provided many photographs of the Thornhill Road Infirmary which have never been published before and also gave me valuable information about the man who took most of them, her grandfather William Gibson, the architect of the Gartcows building. Finally I would like to thank the staff at Falkirk Archives in Callendar House and Geoff Bailey, Keeper of Archaeology and Local History, for their help. Despite all of this assistance, there will no doubt be some errors and omissions and these are my responsibility alone.

I.S.

CHAPTER ONE

A World Ill-divided

In 1797, as the momentous 18th century was drawing to a close, the Minister of Falkirk, Dr James Wilson, wrote a long and detailed description of his huge parish for the famous Statistical Account of Scotland. Drawing attention to the rapid rise in population and the changing character of the community he attributes the 'astonishing improvements' to the establishment of the mighty ironworks at Carron in 1759 and the cutting of the 'Great Canal' from Forth to Clyde two decades later. Together these had set in train the transformation of Falkirk district from a quiet agricultural community into a powerhouse of the industrial revolution. Workers and their familes freed from the land by the revolution in agriculture had come to the old burgh and the surrounding villages from all over Scotland and beyond drawn by the prospect of hard but steady work. Small semi-rural settlements like Stenhousemuir, Grahamston, Bainsford and Camelon expanded to accommodate the newcomers and, all over the district, mining villages were born to satisfy the seemingly insatiable demand for fuel from the hungry furnaces. In the century before 1850 the population of Falkirk Parish rose from 4,000 to over 17, 000 and the newcomers found themselves crammed into common lodging houses and hastily erected buildings without the most basic facilities. Though there were a number of doctors in private practice whose services were available to those who could afford to pay, medical care for the vast majority was almost non existent at the very time when overcrowding and lack of proper housing, sanitation and supplies of clean water were stoking up the fires of fever and infectious disease. Surrounded as they were by the belching fumes of foundries, mines and brickworks it is no surprise that life expectancy at birth for a man was less that 40 and only slightly better for women. However, the idea of intervention by Government, at either local or national level, to rectify this situation

Falkirk town centre around 1830

was anathema to the middle class entrepreneurs and men of business who promoted the new industrial enterprises. Indeed for the most part they maintained this hostility to taxation being used as a means of funding reforms right through the 19th century and almost every new initiative which required such intervention was strenuously resisted. Even the spectre of regular fever epidemics did not move many from this entrenched position. However the ravages of a nation-wide cholera epidemic in 1832 seems to have been the catalyst for action at last and the authorities at national level began to gather information from towns and cities in a first attempt to understand the nature of the fevers and propose action for their prevention. Once cholera arrived in a community it was transmitted in the main by drinking water contaminated by human waste and in Falkirk the conditions were ripe for rapid spread with deadly results. In England the great reformer Edwin Chadwick reported on the sanitary conditions of working communities in 1840. This pointed the way to major public works — water supplies, sewerage systems and the like — but in Scotland it was the regular visits of typhus which most exercised the minds of the medical fraternity. Typhus was a fever transferred from person to person by a louse which found a warm welcome in overcrowded places and among undernourished and poorly clad people. In Falkirk in 1843, Dr George Hamilton was in no doubt where the problems lay:

> The lodging houses are the most fertile sources of fever . . . we have sometimes in them a succession of fever cases in the same bed; one person is seized, another dies or is removed, another is received into the same house and bed, is attacked in the same manner, and gives way to a successor who receives the same infection. I have known these houses to be the means through vagrants of introducing fever from Glasgow and other parts.

And it was not only the impoverished and weak that were carried off in this way:

> I certainly hold that destitution is favourable to the diffusion of fever, but I have observed that the strongest and most worthy labourers, in full employment, have been attacked with fever when they came into contact with these centres, as it were, of poison.

Reports like this certainly helped focus the minds of the powers-that-be and led, not without the usual arguments and resistance, to the establishment of Parochial Boards in every Scottish parish in 1845 to replace the centuries old and completely inadequate system of managing poor relief and dealing with matters of community health and well-being. This Poor Law Amendment Act had far reaching consequences for industrial towns throughout Scotland and set in train a sequence of events that eventually overcame the worst defects. The Boards were given the power to raise finance through local rates for the relief of poverty and where necessary to provide medicines and the services of doctors. In Falkirk the new Board made an early and, what turned out to be an inspired appointment which ensured that the town and surrounding area would not be left behind in tackling the most urgent of its problems. In 1847 John Beeby was appointed as clerk to the Board's Collector of Rates and three years later Inspector of Poor, a position he retained for 56 years. Although originally from Broxburn, he had been educated in the Falkirk Parish School and for half a century he inspired, bullied and cajoled the reluctant burghers into introducing far-reaching changes. For this he deserves to be remembered as one of

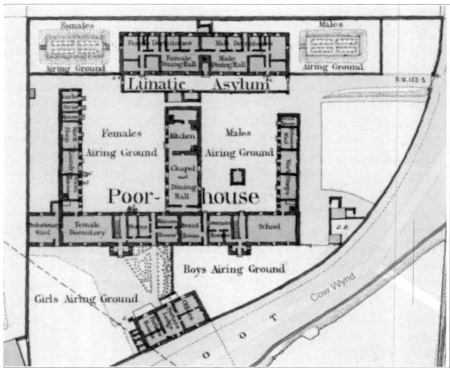

Falkirk Poor's House and Lunatic Asylum

Falkirk's greatest public servants though he is seldom mentioned when the roll of honour is compiled. One of John Beeby's earliest initiatives led directly to the establishment of what was the town's first hospital.

In 1847 a particularly bad outbreak of fever among workers on the new Midland Junction Railway caused serious alarm and Beeby proposed to the Board that they should respond by building a Fever Hospital funded by the assessments allowed by the Act of Parliament. Despite protests at the costs involved this went ahead and, three miles to the south of the town at Lochgreen, and well away from the populous area, on the ancient common lands of the burgh arose Falkirk's first ever hospital. It was a small structure of wood and slate intended to be a temporary measure until the fever abated. Although a pathetically small response to the overwhelming threat from the ever present fevers it was a beginning. But in the years that followed little more was done until the town once again faced a major fever outbreak in the 1860s when the hospital was refurbished with bricks and mortar replacing some but not all of the original wooden building.

Back in 1850 John Beeby brought forward another proposal. The Board had expressed alarm at the growing level of poverty in the parish and were anxious to reduce the bill for poor relief. Beeby's answer was to provide Falkirk with a new Poor's House incorporating an 'Asylum for Lunatic Paupers'. Here the indigent elderly and the 'deserving poor' could find accommodation, adequate food and, crucially, the attentions if required of a doctor appointed by the Board. Although there was no dedicated hospital section as there would be eight years later in Stirling, there is no doubt that nurses of some kind were employed and basic care made available. The building had mens' and womens' sections each with their own exercise area and stood on the corner of Cow Wynd and High Station Road where Comely Park School is today. It continued to serve as the Poor's House until 1905 when some of Falkirk's more sensitive souls objected to its presence in the centre of the town and it was relocated to what later became Blinkbonny Home and still later, Windsor Hospital. The High Station Road building served thereafter as a home for the elderly, a working man's hostel and, after World War II, the County Trades School where apprentice joiners, painters, bricklayers and plasterers acquired their skills until Falkirk College opened in the early 1960s.

Another of John Beeby's proposals was for the creation of a parish cemetery to replace the overcrowded churchyards which were yet another danger to health. As a result of his promptings the Parochial Board acquired land at Dorrator and in 1870 the present cemetery was opened. Thereafter burials in the churchyards declined though it was some time before the threat to public health from this source was removed completely.

Although the establishment of the Fever Hosptal, the Poor's House and the Cemetery were examples of enlightened self interest there is no doubt that there was in mid-Victorian Scotland a change of attitude and a new approach to social problems which was a characteristic of the age. No doubt this was in part at least the impact of rapidly spreading disease – no respecter of class or condition – which threatened the very survival of the businessmen themselves as well as their firms and families but there was more to it than this. Back in 1842 the Westminster Parliament had reported on the condition of women and children in mines and foundries, and the coal and iron masters of Falkirk district were not exempt from the withering criticism levelled at the employers throughout the land. People were shocked at the stories of five and six year old children labouring in dark and dank coal mines and the illiterate boy moulders at Carron facing death or serious injury for long hours everyday untouched by education or the influence of the church. Not long after the passing of the Act which ended such practices, Scotland experienced a great Disruption in the church which brought to life the Free Church of Scotland with a new emphasis on evangelising those it saw as languishing in poverty and ignorance of the scriptures. New thoughts on what constituted a Christian's duty towards the poor and abandoned became widespread in the years after 1843 and this was fundamental to what was to follow.

Increasingly too there was a new sense of municipal pride and, as the district grew more affluent, the thoughts of many turned to the general state of the town and its suburbs, especially those most affected by the rise of industry like Grahamston and Bainsford. From 1850 on a group of forward looking citizens tried to promote a special Act of Parliament which would grant to the almost impotent Town Council the powers to improve the water supply, sanitation, paving, lighting and policing of the district. Men like Provost Thomas Kier, Free Church Minister Rev Lewis Hay Irving and Surgeon James Girdwood argued passionately that the town had the money and must use it to bring about change. The dispute went all the way to the Houses of Parliament and in both Lords and Commons the sorry tale of Falkirk's deteriorating condition, the plight of the sick and poor, the lack of facilities and the inability to agree among themselves was played out in full public gaze. Dr Girdwood pointed out that the mortality rate in Falkirk was the highest of any town of comparable size in Scotland, and higher even that the City of Edinburgh:

> The cholera was fatal in the ill-drained localities of the town such as Kerse Lane and the Howgate. In 1847 there was a visitation of typhus fever. One house alone [in Wooer Street] had fifty cases of fever.

Rev Irving described Falkirk High Street in scathing terms:

> Many houses are totally unfit for human habitation. In the low crowded houses fevers of the typhoid character are prevalent. The ground of the churchyard is black animal soil the produce of decomposition and it is from one to nine feet above adjoining houses. The drainage from the churchyard into a ditch which receives also the refuse matter from the houses produces an abominable compound and in the neighbourhood typhoid fever often resulting fatally occurs.

And Procurator Fiscal John Gair was equally shocked:

> We have only one sewer. This is in the main street and it gets choked up for the want of water to flush it. There are very few water closets and the town therefore presents a most disgusting appearance especially the bye streets. Away from the causeway road there are nuisances before every door lying there for days together. The filth of Falkirk has become a byeword among all who have known it.

As well as evidence of Falkirk's sanitary condition the proposers complained of the inadequate supply of water, the lack of proper policing, the state of the roads and the shortage of street lighting.

The Bill would give the Town Council the power to raise the revenue to address all of these. But there was a powerful group both inside and outside the Council who opposed the measure with equal enthusiasm. They had no intention of paying high taxes to fund improvements which they thought were not necessary. Medical men came forward to deny some of the dire health warnings and other leading lights in the community were ready to argue that Falkirk was as neat and clean a town as one could find anywhere in the kingdom. Having listened to a description of Bainsford one shocked Lord said it sounded like the garden of Eden, which the witness did not dispute! In the end the Lords and MPs decided in favour of the proposers and in September 1859 the Falkirk Police and Improvement Act was passed into law.

The transformation of Falkirk was possible at last but it was a slow process made more difficult by the acceleration in the growth of the town and the surrounding district. Twenty new foundries opened their doors before 1880 and no corner of East Stirlingshire was left untouched. Bonnybridge, Denny, Laurieston and Larbert all joined in the scramble to cash in on the world demand for high quality cast iron goods, both domestic and military, and, as before, little thought was given to the miserable conditions in which the new workforce were forced to live. The population of Falkirk parish doubled between 1850 and the end of the century and many of the old problems of poor housing, overcrowding, sickness and disease remained. However improvement did come. Efforts were made to improve the water supply, streets were cleaned, the worst slums cleared and common lodging houses were regulated. John Beeby and the Parochial Board oversaw the introduction of various Acts of Parliament like the 'Nuisances Act' which sought to end the accumulations of human and animal waste which were common everywhere in the streets and often inside the houses. Compulsory vaccination of children was introduced in 1855 and adults were encouraged to follow suit. A Medical Officer was appointed with responsibility for the general health of the population though once again his efforts were inhibited by the reluctance of the powers-that-be to vote sufficient funding. Gradually the killer infectious diseases were reduced and then eliminated though they were replaced by increasing outbreaks of scarlet fever, whooping cough, diptheria and tuberculosis.

The 1881 building at Lochgreen pictured around 2004

In 1880 John Beeby urged the Parochial Board to do something about the Fever Hospital which was, he said, a disgrace to a prosperous town like Falkirk. It was dilapidated and there were only two wards, one for each sex which meant that infectious and non-infectious patients had to share the same accommodation. Despite the opposition of many the Board agreed to replace the buildings at Lochgreen with a new hospital building which opened in 1881. But if the Board thought that providing a new building was all that was required they were wrong. We are fortunate that a handwritten report of an inspection visit to the Hospital has survived in the former Central Region Archives in Stirling. Dated 16th January 1889 and signed by Dr Henry Littlejohn from Edinburgh it describes in some detail his visit to the hospital a few days earlier as well as the inspection of some common lodging houses. After praising the new accommodation as well-planned and furnished, and located in 'a breezy situation' he goes on:

I found the Superintendent James Laing on duty together with two elderly females as assistants who were occupied in the kitchen and in ordinary cleaning. There were only 3 patients under treatment viz: two females (mother and daughter) and one adult male — all convalescent from typhus fever and making a satisfactory recovery.

The wards were clean and well aired; and I observed that one of the female occupants (the daughter) had just finished washing the floor of her ward.

One of the female assistants had a few days before been sent up from the Poorshouse. She stated to me that she had acted as a ward attendant in Queensberry House, Edinburgh. Mr Laing, the Superintendant, informed me that he it was who administered the medicines to the patients of both sexes by night and by day.

Dr Littlejohn then reports that the patients are happy with their care though a widow he met later in the day did complain about the treatment her late husband had received at Lochgreen. He concluded that with the existing staff it was impossible to treat an 'exacting' disease like typhus:

There may be some excuse for the employment of unskilled Poorhouse Nurses for such chronic ailments as Bronchitis and other infirmities of old age, but infectious diseases require for their proper treatment thoroughly skilled nursing.

He recommended that if there were any more typhus cases then a skilled nurse should be brought from Glasgow or Edinburgh immediately. Turning his attention to the common lodging houses he described one in the Back Row (now Manor Street) as unfit for human habitation which had recently been closed down by the authorities. Many of the rest were hardly much better and none had 'any privy or WC accommodation'. 'Indeed' he said, 'Falkirk appears to be very defficient in the matter of public conveniences of any kind'

Before leaving the town Dr Littlejohn met up with Dr Joseph Peake, the Medical Officer of the Parish and Burgh and visiting physician at the Fever Hospital:

To my surprise I learned that he had no fixed salary for his Public Health duties or for his attendance at the Hospital but that he was paid for each piece of professional work, eg he received 5 shillings for each visit paid to the Hospital. He did, therefore, not feel called upon to inspect the Common Lodging Houses or indeed any nuisance unless specially desired to do so by the Local Authority. I cannot but consider this a most unsatisfactory state of matters and am clearly of the opinion that Falkirk is a burgh of sufficient importance to warrant its possessing the salaried services of a Medical Officer of Health. The history of the present Epidemic, the imperfect hospital management and the condition of the Common Lodging Houses conclusively show the advantages that would have accrued to Falkirk had the responsibility of watching over the sanitary condition of this important centre of communication between the east and the west of Scotland been entrusted to such an official.

Even without such a formal appointment Dr Peake was not short of work. Just a year before the visitation the *Falkirk Mail* of March 1888 reported that:

the public vaccinator Dr Peake will make a house to house visitation in the rural villages for the purpose of making enquiries as to parties requiring vaccination or revaccination and will perform such gratuitously.

The same issue of the newspaper noted that the Sanitary Inspector would set out to find those who failed to manage their 'piggaries, dungsteads and privies' in a proper fashion.

Just a year after Dr Littlejohn's visit Parochial Boards were replaced by County Councils and the Fever Hospital was purchased by the Town Council and became, of course, the Burgh or 'High Hospital' at Lochgreen which served the community for the best part of 150 years. With the Fever Hosptal now the exclusive property of the burgh, the communities outside the town in the rest of East Stirlingshire were left without a facility of their own and this was rectified in 1896 by the opening in Camelon of a fine new hospital which served until 1958 when it became a centre for adults with learning difficulties. It is presently used by the Social Work department.

It would be fair to say that, despite the findings of Dr Littlejohn, Falkirk had come a long way in the second half of the 19th century and many of the killer diseases had been banished. A new water supply to the town opened in 1891 and provided over 40 gallons of fresh water per person per day and this perhaps, more than anything else, contributed to the rise in life expectancy.   But in a rapidly growing industrial community there were many other threats to health than fever. Foundries and mines were dangerous places, and the areas in which they were located were unhealthy environments in which to live and raise families. Increasingly the thoughts of the great and the good turned to the plight of those caught up in industrial accidents or whose general health brought misery to themselves and their children. A few weeks after Dr Littlejohn's visit Falkirk's first Infirmary, the little Cottage Hospital in Thornhill Road, was officialy opened and that is the next part of the story.

CHAPTER TWO

The Cottage Hospital

Despite the real improvements which followed the passing of the 1859 Act, the late Victorian world remained a harsh and ill-divided place for the vast majority of Falkirk bairns. Indeed the growing prosperity earned on the fertile carse-lands to the north and east, and by unrivalled skill in ironfounding, served to widen the gap between the haves and the have nots and only the prospect of steady though hard and heavy work kept the spectre of poverty from the doors of the Garrison, the Back Row or the Howgate and from the overcrowded closes of Bainsford and Grahamston.

At the other end of the social scale, in the comfortable villas of Arnothill, Gartcows and Bantaskine, or in the fine mansion houses scattered throughout East Stirlingshire, gentlemen and their families enjoyed the fruits of successful business and industry. Ironmasters and lawyers, landowners and brewers; gentlemen from Millfield and Carronpark, from Parkhill House, Arnotdale and Powfoulis; the Cockburns and Wilsons, Dawsons, Steins and Forbes, Gibsons and Aitkens, Russels and Mitchells — along with those classified in one local index as 'nobility, gentry, clergy and private residents'.

As the century wore on such people, in Falkirk district as elsewhere in Britain, increasingly acknowledged that wealth and power brought with them a duty to help ameliorate the condition of the poorest in society. The discharge of this 'duty' found its expression in a host of charitable works which later generations would find patronising but which were, for the most part, motivated by a genuine desire to help. Such activities were in marked contrast to their long standing hostility to direct intervention by local or national government and to the additional rates burden that came with it. That position remained unchanged but voluntary giving was different and was the key to much of what was achieved in the last years of the 19th century.

It was the wives and daughters of the families — the 'ladies' — who led the way and by the 1880s their efforts, most often turned to the plight of the sick-poor, regarded as 'deserving', that is, those whose difficulties were not thought to be the result of idleness or improvidence. And there were many men, women and children whose lives were devastated by the injury or illness of the bread-winner in an era before welfare benefits provided a safety net. For the victims there was little help available beyond the support of a close community of fellow-workers assisted by the occasional generous doctor, prepared to offer free medicine and treatment to the poorest and most defenceless. Although a growing number of working men did contribute a few pennies each week to schemes of insurance aimed at providing some kind of medical care many had to rely on the vast array of quack medicines on offer in the columns of the *Falkirk Herald* every week promising cures for everything from dyspepsia to lumbago or even cancer. For the rest there was nothing to be done but await the steady decline into poverty and the prospect of an early grave.

Foremost amongst the ladies who turned their attention to this problem was Mrs Harriette Gibson the wife of John E Gibson of Camelon Ironworks. Mrs Gibson was born into a wealthy and influential family in England but by the mid-century her father had fallen from favour and the young Harriette's prospects were poor. Her determination to make her own way led her to Scotland as a Governess in Helensburgh after which she answered an advertisement for a similar post placed by John Gibson, then working as a Manager in Camelon Foundry. He had recently come to the town from Glasgow and had with him several younger brothers and sisters for whom he was responsible. Their new governess must have made a fine impression because it was not long before she was Mrs Gibson and ready to take her place in Falkirk society alongside her husband who grew wealthy as Camelon Foundry prospered. By the 1880s her influence in the town was considerable and she was able to use it to good effect to mobilise support for her plans to help the sick poor. The earliest initiatives were certainly hers and, for nearly forty years, she devoted herself tirelessly to the cause of health care in Falkirk.

It began with regular visits to the homes of the sick in the town and this exposed her to wide-spread suffering and deprivation and convinced her that properly organised health care was essential, and that providing it was the Christian duty of all. Then out of the blue, in April, 1884 a letter appeared in the *Falkirk Herald* from a wealthy Falkirk exile in England, Mr T M Russell, who offered to donate a sum of money, 'enough to yield £100 per annum for work among the deserving poor in the extension of God's kingdom'. It was exactly the trigger Mrs Gibson required. The following week the paper printed a letter in which she made two suggestions. Firstly, that the money on offer be used to pay for the services of a trained nurse who would,

> . . . . go from house to house, make beds, wash the patients, dress sores, remove all offensive matter from the rooms, prepare food and by her example stimulate those about her to keep things in order.

The response was swift and from an important source. Dr Joseph Peake a local practitioner in Woodlands who was, as we have already noted, Falkirk's Medical Officer, public vaccinator and Fever Hospital physician, was fullsome in his support not only for the likely health benefits, but because, 'it would also tend to inculcate habits of prudence and forethought amongst the working classes'. In the weeks and months which followed letters of encouragement and offers of support multiplied, and by the end of the year Mrs Gibson was ready for the next step. On January 29th 1885, along with a group of ladies of her acquaintance, she formed an 'Association for the Providing of Trained Nurses for the Sick' and, shortly afterwards, on the advice of Dr Joseph Bell, appointed Miss Annie Joss of Edinburgh as the first visiting nurse. With the support of James Wilson of North Bantaskin, Mrs Gibson now established a branch of the St Andrew's Ambulance Association in the town with the good lady herself acting as Secretary for the ladies' classes

Miss Annie Joss

and a Mr T M Watson, later a G.P in the USA, looking after the gentlemen! Miss Joss began her work in the community assisted by the ladies of the Association, and by 1887 had helped over 200 patients 'being instrumental in raising several families out of great misery'. But this was only the beginning.

Mrs Gibson had already signalled her main objective in that first letter to the *Herald*:

> In conclusion let us hope that another year will not pass without our making an effort to have some place, though it were only one room with a few beds, where accidents could be attended to without causing the poor sufferer the added pain incurred by a journey to Edinburgh or Glasgow.

Now Mrs Gibson put pen to paper once again. What better way of celebrating the forthcoming jubilee of Queen Victoria's reign than by establishing a Victoria Cottage Hospital? The want of such a place was 'a shame and a disgrace to the locality' and if the gentlemen and working people of Falkirk would provide the wherewithal she and her ladies would pledge their efforts as collectors, visitors, providers and supporters to the institution. Again the response was very positive and by October 1887 a Committee of Management was established representing many of the most powerful and influential interests in the district. An appeal for funds was launched which within five months had raised £1,300. In March Falkirk's leading architect William Black was invited to design a fourteen-bed building and a few weeks later he looked at the site of Salton Park Cottage in Thornhill Road. The cottage and adjacent land was on offer for £275 and seemed ideal for the purpose. In July 1888, Dr Henry Littlejohn from Edinburgh, whose scathing report on Falkirk we have already encountered, visited the site and concluded:

> I have rarely seen a site so near a populous place yet so retired and so little exposed to objections from neighbouring tenants.

He may have been right in his evaluation of the site but his assessment of the neighbours was well wide of the mark! There was a furious response from local property owners who took the strongest possible exception to a hospital for the poor in their neighbourhood.

Mrs Gibson and Salton Park Cottage

All kinds of objections were advanced. The smoke and smell from a
brickworks close by would not be healthy, surely? The local children
are very noisy – this would disturb the patients, would it not? And
more significantly, our property values will be lowered by the proximity
of the hospital! A petition demanding a new site was circulated, and a
vitriolic campaign supported by Mr Fred Johnston, proprietor and
publisher of the *Falkirk Herald* got underway with an editorial blasting
those 'secretive men' who, behind closed doors, had developed a
scheme to site the hospital 'a respectable distance from Arnothill'.
Mr Johnston, of course, lived at Woodville in nearby Ladysmill and
obviously had a vested interest to defend! A stormy and ill-tempered
meeting of the Committee was held in July at which the proposal to
site in Thornhill was approved by nine votes to three with eighteen
people declining to vote! But it was enough! The scheme went ahead

and the *Herald* thundered its anger and disapproval:

> The hospital has started very inauspiciously in having the
> opposition of the entire district in which it is to be placed and the
> adverse feeling of a large section of the general public who will be
> looked to for its future support.

Despite this, work began almost immediately and continued
throughout the winter and spring of 1889. Mr Black had produced a
plan for a two-storey building behind the original cottage with a female
ward on the ground floor and a male ward above. The building and
equipment costs were £1,050 well within the funding total already
raised.

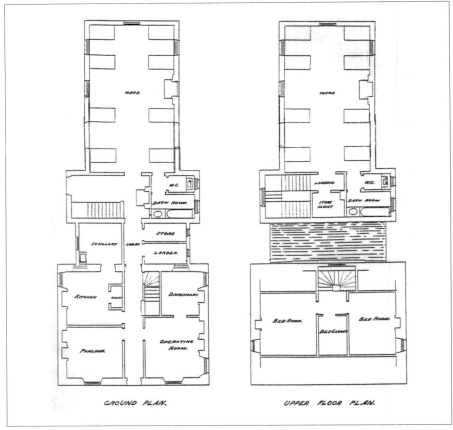

William Black's plan for the new hospital

Falkirk Herald

SATURDAY, JULY 27, 1889.

Public and General Notices.

FALKIRK COTTAGE HOSPITAL.

THE HOSPITAL will be Declared OPEN by T. D. BRODIE, Esquire of Gairdoch, Idvies, &c, TO-DAY (SATURDAY, 27th inst.), at Three o'clock Afternoon.

JAMES WILSON, Esquire of Bantaskin, in the Chair.

The Hospital will be open for Inspection after the Opening Ceremony ; and the Directors will be very glad that all Subscribers and the Public generally should take this opportunity of visiting it.

THOS. GIBSON, Hon. Secy.

National Bank Buildings.
Falkirk, 22nd July, 1889.

FALKIRK BURGH SC

NORTHERN PUBL

ALTERATIONS being CO? SCHOOL, with Accomm Pupils, will be OPEN for PUB SATURDAY, 3rd August, from master will Enrol Pupils on that THOS.
Falkirk D
National Bank Buildings.
Falkirk, 22nd July, 1889.

GRANGEMOUTH DISTRI

RE-OPENING OF
The PUBLIC SCHOOLS will

The original cottage to which the new block was connected contained the Matron's residence, parlour, kitchen, dispensary and operating room on the ground floor with two bedrooms above. In the corner of the garden a small single storey building with wash-house, laundry, coalhouse and mortuary was constructed. Despite the dire warnings financial support for the project continued to increase and soon £1,593 had been raised. Mrs Gibson's dream was coming close to reality. By the summer the hospital was ready and Miss Joss was appointed Matron with the support of two trained nurses. Dr Peake was invited to become the first Medical Officer, a non-residential post which entailed almost daily visits to the Institution. On Saturday, 27th July, before a 'large and brilliant gathering' watched by 'a curious crowd of spectators attracted by the long string of carriages', Mr Thomas Dawson Brodie of Gairdoch and Idvies (and importantly of Carron Company) declared the new Falkirk Cottage Hospital open. Much of the rancour which had accompanied the planning disappeared in the wave of enthusiasm with which the gentry of Falkirk greeted their new acquisition. Outside, as the last of the carriages departed, those less fortunate responded in like manner. ' In the evening', declared one observer, 'a very large number of the working classes inspected the building'. 'Argos' the *Herald*'s commentator on all current affairs, thought the building a bit disappointing on the outside but much better within, except for the decoration:

> Perhaps the wards of our Cottage Hospital would be even more beautiful not to say comfortable but for the numerous scriptural texts displayed on the walls. It is questionable whether it would not be better if some of them were replaced by objects a little more pleasing to the eye and savouring more of this world than the next. However, this is a hobby which good people will have, and is purely a matter of opinion.

He was no doubt referring here to the large framed biblical inscriptions which were one of many gifts given to the new hospital, including ironware, earthenware and 'two gallons of cod liver oil'.

Three days later, on 30th July, a seventeen year old moulder called Patrick Tully with burns on his right foot was admitted as the first ever patient. He was treated with 'Carron Oil', a concoction originally developed at the works and by then in widespread use across the country. One week after that, the mustard plasters were out for Annie Shirra, a domestic servant with bronchitis, who arrived to join him. From then on, admissions were fairly regular adding up to twenty-four in the first year of operation. The report of the Medical Officer, Dr Joseph Peake, on that first year (reproduced on the page opposite) shows the wide range of conditions suffered by the patients on admission as well as the outcomes which were generally satisfactory. Elsewhere in the report the M.O. acknowledges the 'valuable services'

The Doctor's Journal: first entry July 30th 1889 and the Carron Oil

GENTLEMEN, — I have the honour to report that during the period from the 30th of July, 1889, when the first patient was admitted to the Hospital, to the 25th of March, 1890, 24 patients have received medical or surgical advice and treatment. The classification of diseases and injuries is as follows:

Diseases of the Chest	2
„ „ Stomach	2
„ „ Kidney	1
„ „ Skin	2
„ „ Spine	1
„ „ Females	1
Rheumatism	1
Burns	3
Ulcers	3
Tumour	1
Wounds	2
Fractures (of Skull 3, of Thigh 1)	4
Wounds of Blood Vessels	1
Total	24
Cured	13
Relieved	3
Died (both within a few hours of admission from severe head injuries)	2
In Hospital, 25th of March, 1890	6
Total	24

The medical and surgical appliances have been kept in good order, and the wards have always presented a clean and tidy appearance. The wants of the patients have been assiduously and carefully attended to by the nursing staff, and the behaviour of the patients has been satisfactory.

JOSEPH PEAKE, Medical Officer.

Medical Officers's first annual report for 1889-1890

Matron Miss Joss with the nursing and domestic staff

rendered by Professor Clark of Glasgow which confirms that, at this time, where cases required complicated surgery, specialists from the big city hospitals were brought through to Falkirk. Despite the gloomy predictions, the arrival of the Cottage Hospital was greeted with universal pleasure throughout the district, and now that it was operational, pledges of financial support increased dramatically. Mrs Gibson and her associates may have thought it a fitting end to their great effort but it was in truth only the beginning.

Over the first few years the numbers of patients increased steadily. The second year brought 37, then 68, 84 and by 1893-94 it had reached 94 along with the first three out-patients. Those who were 'infectious, incurable or insane' were specifically excluded and non-emergency cases required to produce a letter of recommendation from a doctor confirming that none of these categories applied! Dr Peake and his successors as Medical Officers made regular visits assisted from time to time by other local practitioners and, as we have seen, occasionally by specialists from Glasgow and Edinburgh.

For her part Miss Joss could call on a powerful Ladies Committee representative of the leading families in the district with the redoubtable Mrs Gibson as Secretary. They made weekly visits to supervise the household and domestic arrangements and the accounts, and to collect weekly payments from those patients who were required by the rules to contribute towards their maintenance'. One can imagine the scene as the elegant Mrs Wilson of Bantaskine, Mrs Fenton-Livingstone of Westquarter or Mrs Forbes of Callendar House moved among the concussed or dyspepsic patients checking out their credentials and gathering a few pennies or shillings for the Treasurer!

The main source of finance was, of course, the subscriptions paid by employers on behalf of their workers or by the workers themselves. Ten shillings was the annual subscription though, for a donation of £10, an individual or firm became life subscribers. The response was impressive with initial subscriptions paying for the cottage, land and new building. Thereafter, over £200 was collected in annual contributions to provide for salaries and day-to-day expenses. It is difficult today to appreciate the monetary value of these contributions — suffice to say that a skilled working man at the time might earn around £60 per annum and a domestic servant less that £20. When a person became a subscriber they would be treated free and could also make one recommendation per annum which had to be countersigned by a doctor. Private patients were also provided for and special facilities were made available though at this time it was unusual for the better-off classes to be treated outside their homes. But while they may not have made use of the hospital's services they were certainly true to their early promises to provide unstinting support. A powerful committee of 'Managers', all male, which included the wealthiest and most influential men in Falkirk district, met regularly to oversee the financial and practical affairs of the institution and it was they who reported annually to meetings of subscribers. Presiding over this committee at the outset was James Wilson of North Bantaskin followed by Sheriff Alexander Moffat of Arnotdale who served for many years and played a significant part in managing the whole complex operation. It is worth noting that Fred Johnston, whose opposition to the location of the Cottage Hospital we have already noted, went on to become on of its greatest supporters serving as a Manager for many years.   Each passing year brought greater and greater financial demands and the variety of ways that money, and help in kind, were collected was quite remarkable. For example, the dedicated 'ladies' divided the area into districts and made regular visits to the houses of the

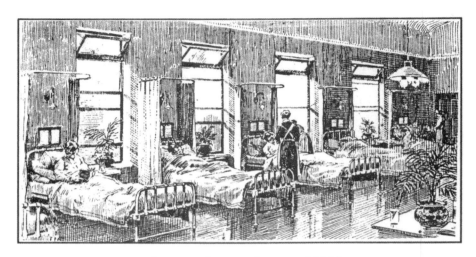

The Female Ward around 1900

well-to-do or business premises soliciting subscriptions or donations of money. Each Annual Report of the Managers list the results of their endeavours. Thus, in 1892, we have the following:

> Collected by Miss Baillie, Carron from J B Sherriff, Carronvale, ten shillings; Reverend J Yellowlees, ten shillings; Mrs Dobbie, Beechmount, ten shillings; William Easton, Carronhall, ten shillings; John J. Cadell, Stenhousemuir, ten shillings; Henry Forrester, Kinnaird, one guinea; sums under five shillings £1.12s.6d.

There were 13 other collectors and the total gathered in was £432.

The local community was encouraged to organise fund raising events, and football matches, concerts and special collections became regular features of town life, providing not only steady income but creating among the people of the district a feeling of pride and ownership which was to play such a crucial part in the developing history of the hospital in the century ahead. Local churches instituted a 'Hospital Sunday' on which the proceeds of special collections were directed specifically to the work of the new hospital. Mrs Gibson's 'ladies' toured the foundries and other workplaces to address groups of workers during their dinner break to plead for financial support in the shape of a penny a week from their wages. Their reception was not always as positive as they would have hoped, as one lady remembers:

My mother was a very elegant lady and always well dressed. She would go to the foundries where she had permission to speak to the men during their dinner break and explain how important it was to subscribe to the hospital. I think some of the men resented a 'posh' lady coming to give them a lecture or maybe they didn't like having their break disturbed, but whatever they would quite often shower her with crusts from their sandwiches. She however was used to this and always carried a parasol which she used to fend of the flying crusts while continuing to exhort the men to support the good cause!

As well as money, gifts in kind were enthusiastically received, and over the years, a staggering volume of goods of every kind imaginable found their way to Thornhill Road for the benefit of the staff and patients. 1897 was typical:

Mrs Carruthers, the Manse — Cast-off clothes, sweets, teabread.
Mrs Adam, Springbank— preserves, flowers, kettle, fireguard.
Mrs Sceales, Thornhill — rhubarb and sugar.
A 'friend' — flannel nightshirts, sox, and slippers.
Rev Ross Taylor — tobacco for men.
Mr Sutherland, Wallside — 6 volumes 'Good Words'.
Mrs Walker, Muirhouse — load of manure, bags of turnips.
Mrs R. Melville & Co. — cart of firewood.

. . . . . . and over 60 other contributions in similar vein. Local clergymen, aided by 'ladies and gentlemen' of the town, held Sunday services in the Hospital to which patients' relatives were invited. These were, or so it was said, greatly appreciated and represented an important aspect of the missionary impulse which was never far from the minds and the lips of the participants in the life of the hospital.

All of these contributions and services were gratefully acknowledged in each Annual Report, which follow a common pattern over the first decade of the Hospital's existence. Each year Miss Joss and her hard pressed staff are lavishly praised for their skill and effort; each year the managers appeal for more and more contributions to keep the hospital afloat, and each year the number of patients sent by their Doctors multiplied. By 1898-9 when the Cottage Hospital reached its 10th

The Medical Officer's Daily Journal 1889
One entry in the second column says

Andrew Somerville 55 years M. Farmer, Wester Broich, Blackburn, Bathgate. Fracture of lower third of left femur caused by a kick from a horse at Falkirk Tryst. Long splint applied. House diet.

anniversary the figure for indoor patients had reached 140 and there were 30 outdoor patients many making multiple visits during the year. Pressure on the accommodation had been felt as early as 1892 when the Managers reported that 'every bed is occupied' and resources were 'stretched to the utmost'. Four years later things were much worse:

The Managers have been pained to find their resources taxed almost beyond what they can bear, and they do trust that in the coming year they may not be brought face to face with the calamity of having to refuse admissions on the grounds that wards are full.

The records actually show that they had already done just that and by 1897 a campaign to extend the hospital was underway:

> The Managers entertain a confident hope that Falkirk will not be behind hand, and that the sixtieth year of the reign of Queen Victoria maybe signalised here by such an addition to the Cottage Hospital as may be no unmeet memorial of so auspicious an event.

That year over £1,800 was subscribed and Mr William Black, designer of the original building, once again offered his services free-of-charge as his contribution. A special endowment fund was established to provide the Hospital with assured future income and soon it was attracting large legacies and donations. We have a tangible reminder of these gifts in the form of the beautiful endowment boards which were once on display in Thornhill Road and now surround the stairwell in the Gartcows Infirmary. It also became fashionable for beds to be endowed in memory of a departed relative or a family or even a family home, and by 1899 the Cottage Hospital had acquired the 'STENHOUSE' bed from Mr George Sheriff of Carronvale and the 'BEECHMOUNT' bed from Major Dobbie. And, in what must be one of the earliest forms of sponsorship, Mr R M Sutherland of Solsgirth endowed the 'LIME WHARF CHEMICAL WORKS' bed, though what the poor occupants made of this is not recorded! Mr Sutherland was one of the Hospital's most generous and faithful benefactors over many year, on one occasion providing the surgery with the most up to date operating instruments then available.

Work on the extension was soon underway and, in the meantime, the medical and caring work of the hospital continued. The rising number of patients had brought in a greatly increased range of ailments and conditions and Dr Peake and his successors Dr Duncan Fraser, Dr George Lesley, Dr James Smith and Dr R D Clarkson deployed a wide variety of surgical and medical techniques. The small sitting-room cum 'theatre' in the old cottage was used more and more for 'chronic ulcers and the extirpation of cancerous growths', as well as skin grafts and many major amputations.

The Medical Officer's Daily Journal for the years 1888 to 1898 has survived and its short handwritten notes on each patient and the treatment given, offer a fascinating picture of the day-to-day life of the

No. of Case	Sex	Age	Occupation	Residence	Disease or Injury	No. of Days in Hospital	Result.
437	M	14	Miner	Shieldhill	Necrosis of tibia	320	Amputation.
445	F	18	Servant	Falkirk	Tuberculous adenitis	31	Improved.
457	F	31	Housewife	Falkirk	Bright's disease	121	Much improved.
467	M	14	Farm Servant	Cauldhame	Lacerated wounds of shoulder	46	Cured.
476	M	28	Labourer	Camelon	Abscess round knee	88	Much improved.
481	F	7		Stenhousemuir	Chorea	44	Cured
490	M	35	Labourer	Falkirk	Fractured leg	48	Recovered.
491	F	5	School Girl	Larbert	Burns of body and arms	91	Cured.
495	F	55	Housewife	Falkirk	Endo-cervicitis	26	Much improved.
496	F	16	Servant	Grahamston	Incipient phthisis	7	Improved.
497	M	18	Moulder	Falkirk	Burnt foot	152	Cured.
500	M	53	Moulder	Falkirk	Cardiac disease	16	Improved
501	M	19	Moulder	Falkirk	Burnt foot	51	Cured.
502	F	18	Housewife	Falkirk	Burnt shoulder		Under treatment.
503	F	8		Forganhall	Lumbar abscess	365	Cured.
504	F	57	Nurse	Larbert	Strangulated hernia	53	Died.
505	F	15	School Girl	Falkirk	Chronic peritonitis	81	Cured.
506	M	28	Furnaceman	West Carron	Breathlessness	19	Left.
507	M	60		Falkirk	Bronchitis	2	Died.
508	M	53	Farm Servant	Falkirk	Valvular heart disease	2	Died.
509	M	23	Cabinetmaker	Grangemouth	Debility albuminuria	28	Much improved.
510	M	54	Housewife	Falkirk	Dilated stomach	21	Cured.
511	M		Labourer	Carronshore	Bronchitis	28	Cured.
512	M		Labourer		Crushed foot	39	Cured.
513	M	23	School Boy	Camelon	Caries	84	Cured.
514	M	0	Chemical Worker	Camelon	Ulcer of leg		Out-door.
515	F		Housewife	Bainsford	General debility	14	Much improved.
516	M	28	Packer	Falkirk	Ulcer of leg	9	Became out door.
517	M	56	Moulder	Falkirk	Cardiac disease	29	Slightly improved.
518	M	53	Moulder	Falkirk	Fracture of leg	49	Cured.
519	F		Housewife	Falkirk	Lupus of face	5	Successful operat.
520	M	54	Shoemaker	Grahamston	Bronchitis	18	Much improved.
521	M	62	Chemical Worker	Camelon	Hemiplegia	8	In statu quo.
522	M	23	Farm Servant	Denny	Compound fracture of femur	74	Cured.

Some of the cases treated in 1897 with the outcomes

Cottage Hospital. The medicines employed, for example, have a homely simplicity to them which seemed to detract not one bit from their effectiveness. Cod liver oil, beef tea, bone lint, castor oil, zinc oxide, boracic acid, charcoal, linseed meal and mustard poultices occur with great regularity. There was brandy and whisky to ease the pain and opium and morphine in extreme cases. On not a few occasions the doctor's recommendation was a straightforward 'dose of salts'. Some of the cases were particularly interesting:

November 2nd 1889.

David Graham age 20 — Butcher — Brought in ambulance waggon from slaughterhouse at 1.00pm. Puncture wound in middle of right thigh involving femerol artery — 5.30pm operation by Professor Clark of Glasgow — thigh amputation.

For young David the diet was much as before — 'Brand's essence of beef, milk and a teaspoon of brandy'.

December 30th 1889.

James Joiner, Larbert admitted — compound fracture of skull. (3 sutures applied to wound over right temple) — thrown out of a trap at Callendar Riggs.

October 14th 1890.

Hugh Milne, 15, Son of a Hawker, admitted with a wound about 5 inches long on the front of the left leg caused by the kick of a horse at Falkirk Tryst.

For most of the patients the clean and pleasant surroundings, good food and rest restored them to health as often as the medicine or the surgeon's knife. Deaths were few and mostly in train before admission.

It was a success story with no parallel in the town's history and the generous response of the community to the extension fund appeal was testimony to the strength of their feeling for 'our hospital'. Work began in 1899 and was completed the following summer. It consisted of a completely new wing built to the north of the hospital building with two new wards, a proper operating room, some much needed extra accommodation for nurses, as well as various ancillary rooms and stores. This more than doubled the capacity to 32 beds and once again the

The Extension building opened in June 1900

gentry turned out in force for the opening ceremony in June 1900. This time it was Lady Dawson Brodie, the widow of Sir Thomas,who did the honours, unlocking the door of the new building with a silver key! There were speeches from half a dozen dignitaries and votes of thanks galore, including a special mention for Mrs Gibson, who replied that:

> It had always given her the greatest of pleasure to do any work in aid of the hospital. It was not everyone who got their heart's desire but the work they had seen completed that day had been hers and she had secured it.

The Victorian era was nearly over. Falkirk entered a new and less certain age with a hospital as good as the best provincial institutions in the country. No one present on that summer day could have guessed that within twelve months the hospital would again be overflowing with patients and that the extension programme, so recently completed, would begin all over again.

CHAPTER THREE

In Peace and War

The year 1900 was the beginning of a new age for the country as well as for Falkirk and its hospital. The old Queen, so long the symbol of the power and influence of Britain and her Empire, was close to death, and Europe was already tense with great powers jostling for position in a deadly game with as yet unimagined consequences. The old supremacy of the 'workshop of the world' was under threat, and the security of working people, never strong, was weaker now than ever.

In Falkirk Mrs Gibson's mind turned back to those who had been her earliest concern back in the the 1880s — the sick poor languishing in their homes, not ill enough to need the hospital but in want of care and attention nonetheless. When the Queen died in 1901 she immediately suggested the formation of a Queen Victoria Memorial Nursing Association for Falkirk. With the help and support of her 'ladies' this was soon operational with premises in Lint Riggs. Two nurses were employed to do what Miss Joss had done so successfully before and during their first year they made 600 visits to homes in and around Falkirk.

At the same time as this new initiative was taking effect, the Cottage Hospital was about to enjoy a decade of phenomenal growth, the result in part of growing recognition on the part of local doctors, employers and employees of the standards of care now available. Nearly 200 patients were admitted in 1900 as well as 100 out-patients attending for minor matters dealt with by the nursing staff. Two significant changes of personnel marked the passing of the early phase of the life of the hospital. In 1899, Dr Alfred Griffiths began a twenty year period of service as the Medical Officer, and his skill as a surgeon helped build a reputation for excellence which attracted many new and more complex cases to Thornhill Road. In June 1902 Miss Joss, Matron for thirteen years, retired and was replaced by Miss Hannah Glendinning,

Miss Glendinning and Dr Griffiths with nurses and visiting doctors

a highly competent and well qualified nursing sister, who also served for twenty years. It was a powerful combination which lifted the Cottage Hospital to a new high level of performance culminating in the important decision of the Managers in May 1904:

> In view of the size of the Hospital, and of the greatly increased importance of the work which is now done there, it is considered that the name Falkirk Cottage Hospital is no longer appropriate and the managers resolved that the name be discontinued and that henceforth the Hospital shall be called the Falkirk Infirmary.

By then there were 355 indoor patients and 202 out-patients, and Dr Griffiths and his associates were conducting more than 250 operations each year, some of them very major and half employing chloroform as a general anaesthetic. On Dr Griffiths recommendation, Dr Shanks was appointed by the managers as an anaesthetist with the additional task of looking after the 'set of Rontgen Rays (cost £49.14s. 9d.)'.   The commitment of those people who had supported the hospital from its foundation was not diminished in any way and the managers, directors, collectors and fundraisers gave up huge amounts of time and material resources to keep their 'creation' strong and viable.

In 1902 Mrs Forbes of Callendar, the Honorary Secretary of the Ladies Committee, paid for 12 women and children patients to have a two week holiday in Chirnside, Berwickshire and the following year her husband gifted the institution an acre of ground behind, and to the east of the buildings, which had been grassed and fenced as a recreational area for convalescing patients.

As early as 1901 the Hospital had again experienced serious overcrowding and, as the years passed and there was no sign of demand decreasing, the Managers decided that only another extension would solve the problem. Mr Forbes' acre now proved a godsend as a site for yet another building. In 1905 at a public meeting, plans for an extension were unveiled and another appeal for funds launched. It goes without saying that the response from the people of Falkirk and district was immediate and substantial, confirming what was already evident, that the Infirmary was now central to the life of the people of the area, a much loved institution on which the expenditure of time and money, once a duty, was now a labour of love. By this time the early reservations about the hospital and its location seem to have disappeared and any doubts that remained were removed by experience as this slightly barbed comment from the Managers in 1905 makes clear:

> In common with all good movements . . . . it has had its detractors, but it is significant that when any of those have had the misfortune to require its aid as patients, they have invariably forgotten to find fault, and have left the place with expressions of the utmost gratitude, and with a determination to take every opportunity to advance its interests in the future.

The growth in the number of children treated led to proposals for a dedicated children's ward and the fund raisers used this in their publicity to attract even more sympathetic responses from the community. A two day concert in the Town Hall billed as 'chidren's offering to the Falkirk Infirmary' performed 'in the presence of the School Board and the Directors of the Infirmary' was an outstanding success and the programme explains just why the new developments were necessary:

During 1905 there were treated at the Infirmary 160 cases of children under 13 years. Of these 63 were under 4 years of age. And some were inmates for from 4 to 5 months. Operations were performed in 68 of these cases.

All classes in the community rallied round and work began in 1905 and was completed the following autumn. The original Salton cottage was demolished to be replaced by a new building containing a larger and better equipped operating theatre, a further eight beds, an administrative area and accommodation for the nursing staff. The gas lighting was replaced by electricity and the main buildings of the hospital were now heated by a hot water pipe system. The new ward was named the 'Mrs J E Gibson Ward' as a tribute to the hospital's founder and guiding spirit and was used exclusively for children. The nurses' accommodation also reflected substantial growth. Miss Glendinning had by 1906 a senior charge nurse, three nurses and two probationers at various stages of training as well as a number of maids and other domestic workers

Over £3,500 was subscribed for the new extension, and many local employees, especially in the foundries, agreed to pay a penny each week for a year to support the work of the Infirmary. Throughout the

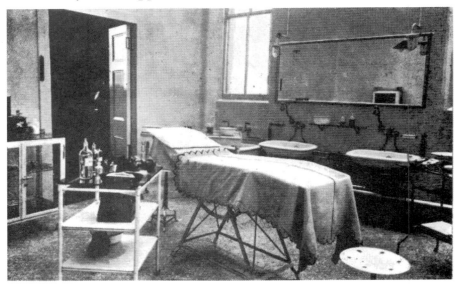

The new Operating Theatre in 1906

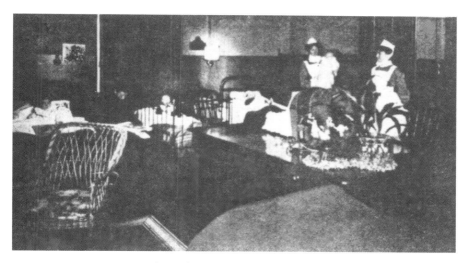

The Childrens' Ward 1906

district the wide range of fund raising events described earlier continued apace and the endowment fund, started in 1898 to provide a secure income for the Infirmary, benefited by a number of substantial legacies.

On the 2nd November 1906, the lines of carriages once again made their way from the mansion houses and villas to Thornhill Road for yet another opening ceremony. This time Miss Dawson of Powfoulis, sister of Lady Brodie and joint inheritor of much of the Carron Company's massive wealth, was invited to declare the new building open. Again there were fine speeches, lavish praise and earnest appeals for further support. It was a happy occasion, and if the 'working classes' remained firmly outside the railings (except those who made and served the tea and dainties!) then it was no more than a feature of the times, still accepted by the 'haves and have nots' alike, however unacceptable it may be in our egalitarian age.

The new operating theatre, fully equipped by an anonymous donor, was the outstanding addition of this particular extension, said by the Managers to be found in no similar institution in Scotland. Certainly Dr Griffiths was delighted and the numbers of operations continued to soar in the months after the new facilities were commissioned. At this time Dr Brown was in charge of both anaesthetics and the X-ray equipment and Dr Griffiths was ever fullsome in his praise of his

Falkirk Infirmary after the completion of the extension in 1906

colleague: 'His skill in both these branches is of the highest and his value to the Infirmary is incalculable' The numbers continued to increase at an astonishing rate and by 1908 nearly 500 'indoor' and a similar number of out-patients were being treated. The following year the old familiar story was heard yet again:

> The accommodation of the Hospital is barely adequate as at times during the year we have had a considerable list of patients who have had to wait.

The Annual Reports for the period provide very detailed accounts of the medical, financial and social life of the Infirmary. Every in-patient is listed and while the names are omitted we are given their age, sex, occupation, nature of sickness or injury, length of stay and outcome. These make fascinating reading and for scholars of health and hospital care they provide a massive amount of very useful data. Among the most surprising statistics are the number of days spent in hospital by many patients with what would appear to us as relatively minor problems. Inguinal hernias for example which are same day operations nowadays often meant anything from 10 to 21 days in hospital and broken legs of which there were many might cause the sufferer to stay in Thornhill Road for up to 60 days! Other examples picked at random from the 1910-11 report were, bruises — 22 days; appendectomy —21 days; haemorrhoids — 17 days; ulcers of leg — 62 days — of those who survived to be cured and discharged, more than 90% had spent more than 10 days in hospital! It was little wonder that there was always a problem of demand out stripping supply and that things continued to get worse as the century advanced.

Two new initiatives at national level placed further strains on the accommodation. In 1911 the Liberal Government introduced a National Health Insurance scheme which, among other things, meant that working people when sick had free access to a panel of doctors. This had the effect of reducing the number of outdoor patients coming to the hospital but in the end greatly increased the number who were diagnosed with serious conditions requiring in-patient treatment. The Government indicated its willingness to pay voluntary hospitals which treated TB patients and this proved a small but welcome source of additional income. Around the same time the health inspection of

Nurses fundraising bazaar in Falkirk Town Hall in April 1910

school children was gradually introduced though the response of the education authorities was patchy to say the least. Again the number of young people requiring in and out-patient treatment increased but this time the authorities were most reluctant to provide funding to support this extra work. This probably contributed to the failure for the first time in the three years 1911-1913, to balance the books and the Managers were forced to use money set aside for future extensions, and even from the endowment fund, to keep things on an even keel. The shortfall figures of around £250-£300 seem small sums to us today but we must bear in mind that the total annual expenditure on the hospital was around £1,500. By 1911 there were over 1,000 patients in total and in 1914 the same number plus 600 operations. Plans were made to create verandahs and a waiting room while increasing the number of beds by 7 but the outbreak of the Great War in August the same year put an end to the plans for the time being.

The difficulties which had plagued the Managers and their hard pressed staff before the war were nothing compared to the massive problem which now faced them. In common with local hospitals throughout the country, Falkirk Infirmary was requested by the War Office to provide for the medical needs of new recruits, as well as wounded soldiers, and the Managers set about the task of reconstructing and extending the Infirmary once again. Falkirk was designated a military hospital attached to Stobhill base hospital in Glasgow and received soldiers from there as required by the authorities. Two new wards each holding twenty beds were constructed in 'temporary' wooden buildings and the first of these was ready by the Autumn. An appeal went out for furniture and fittings and over time a number of big houses were lent by their owners for use as hospital annexes with accommodation for patients or nursing staff. Wallside in Camelon and Hillside on Arnothill became Auxiliary Hospitals and Kersehill House in Grahamston was put to use as nurses home. The Marquis of Zetland provided 30 beds and bedding and the British Red Cross Society added mattresses, pillows, sheets etc. In November 1914 the first of many hundreds wounded on the western front arrived at Grahamston Station en route for Thornhill Road, among them three Belgians wounded in the gallant stand against the advancing German army in the very first days of the conflict.

Although the first arrivals were followed by many others described in the records as 'overseas man – gunshot wounds', 'overseas man – shrapnel wound', the vast majority were Territorials recruited locally whose medical examinations, perhaps their first ever, had revealed conditions requiring treatment before they could be sent off to the trenches. Falkirk Infirmary's role, at least in the early years, was more one of preparing than repairing and the list of conditions among the men make interesting reading. Up to February 1915, for example, there were 33 overseas soldiers treated for fractures and bullet wounds as well as bronchitis, rheumatism, frost-bite and ague. In the same period 184 territorials were in-patients suffering from anaemia, sciatica, rheumatism, haemorrhoids, varicose veins, hernia, flat feet, hammer toes, scabies, eczema, psoriasis and tonsilitis. The surgeon was also busy – '62 operations were performed on soldiers to fit them for active service and 50 operations have been performed to enable men to enlist'. Dr Griffiths was not in doubt of the value of the service provided:

> These figures should be very gratifying to the managers and the public of Falkirk who subscribe to the funds of the Infirmary. To be useful to the sick and wounded at a time of such great national emergency is one of the greatest rewards the public spirited people of this district could have had. The Infirmary I am satisfied has done as good a national service as some of the biggest hospitals in the Kingdom.

As the number of military patients increased there was an obvious reduction in space available for civilians but this was offset to some extent by the numbers of men leaving the district to join the forces. Inevitably then the war years were dominated by the treatment of military personnel – over 1,800 had been admitted by the end of hostilities in 1918. In 1915 the figure was 534, well over half the patients in that year. One recurring problem which was never really solved related to the convalescence of soldiers treated in the Infirmary. At an early stage the managers provided a wooden recreation building and also used the hall of nearby St James Church until, thanks to the generosity of Mr Thomas McGill of Callander, they were able to send soldiers to Inverleny House which was made an official annexe of Falkirk Infirmary staffed by the volunteers from Callander Red Cross supported by local doctors as required. This proved a great boon but, for undisclosed reasons, in December, 1916 the military authorities insisted that the arrangement be ended. Perhaps the beautiful scenery, country air and other local attractions proved too distracting to young men preparing for a return to the mud of Flanders? Whatever the reason, the Managers in Falkirk responded by purchasing the East Stirlingshire Cricket Club Pavilion for £150 and installing it in Thornhill Road. At the same time an urgent request from the Red Cross for more beds for soldiers led to the conversion of the existing recreation hut into a new ward with forty additional beds.

From the outset it was clear that the existing handful of nursing staff could not cope with the greatly increased workload and, since qualified nurses were required elsewhere, an appeal was made for volunteers to:

> Give gratuitously twelve hours duty in the Infirmary daily on the footing of probationers for a minimum of one month.

The Falkirk and Larbert Voluntary Aid Detachment of the Red Cross – the famous VADs – responded to this and over the next few years fifty five of their number nursed the soldiers under the direction of the Matron Miss Glendinning. As one of the Managers commented later, 'Their services were given entirely gratutously and the Doctor and the Matron speak in high terms of the manner in which they have performed their duties'. Without their contribution the work of the Infirmary would certainly have ground to a halt, especially since the continuation of the war saw more and more of the qualified

nurses leave to serve in military hospitals at home and overseas. In early 1916 for example, Sister Harper, the most senior nurse in the Infirmary, left for service in Salonica at a time when the number of patients was at the highest level of the war years.

Wartime fund raising rally at the Town Hall.
Mrs Gibson is sitting to the right of the speaker

The doctors too were in demand elsewhere. Dr Wallace, assistant physician, was called up in August, 1914 and a year later Dr Griffiths himself accepted a commission in the RAMC and went south to a large military hospital in England. A number of local doctors including former Medical Officers Fraser and Clarkson stepped into the breach and the work continued, though the Managers did express grave concern at their ability to carry the increased workload. In late 1917 a new arrangement was introduced in which Dr Fraser became Consulting Physician mainly responsible for the military patients, Mr Wilkie from Edinburgh came through each week to do the major operations and, significantly as it turned out, a new face, that of Dr Andrew Hunter took over as Assistant Surgeon and Physician. For Dr Hunter it was the start of an unbroken spell of distinguished service and his name will figure largely in the story of the growth and development of Falkirk Infirmary over the following thirty years. In his excellent account of Falkirk at war called 'Heroes Departed' published back in 1994, John Dickson tells us that

> From an early stage of the war convalescent soldiers in 'hospital blues' became a familiar sight in Falkirk. These were distinctive bright blue uniforms, cut like civilian suits and worn with a red tie.

He recounts the story of Trooper Arthur Sykes who was so pleased with his treatment at the hands of the Falkirk Infirmary staff that he sent a letter with a cartoon to the *Falkirk Herald* which was published in October 1917 and is reproduced below with permission.

This is no real surprise because, for the well-to-do, with both time and money available, the sight of soldiers wounded on patriotic duty released a frenzy of extra charitable activity, and the Infirmary was swamped with gifts for the men as the list on page 44 shows. In the

WOUNDED TOMMY'S TRIBUTE TO FALKIRK

The above local topical sketch was specifically drawn and sent us by Tropper Arthur Sykes (Duke of Lancaster's Yeomanry) who has been a convalescent patient at Falkirk Infirmary for some time past. Trooper Sykes is high in his praise of the Falkirk people for their kindness and hospitality to the wounded in their midst.

first year of the war for example, 118 groups or individuals sent in gifts including hundreds of pairs of socks, bedjackets, slippers, boots, cigarettes, tea, books, magazines, bananas, rabbits, and a vast quantity of cast-off clothing including underwear! Some gifts were, however, aimed directly at the foreign guests:

> Master Gibson, Hodge Street — two scarves for the Belgians. Mr and Mrs Jack, Kerse Lane — pair of chickens for the Belgians. Mrs Dobbie, Larbert — two boxes of shortbread for the Belgians.

Other presents were larger and more prominent like the fifty- foot flagstaff gifted by Muirheads of Grangemouth which decorated the front entrance to the Infirmary thereafter. It was to signify much more than victory in the war for, with so much death and destruction where was the victory? Much more than this, it symbolised the way in which the Infirmary had come through its first major test with colours flying, but the peace was hardly a year old when familiar problems returned. But in the immediate aftermath of peace the Infirmary and especially the matron received much praise for their contribution to the war effort with Miss Glendinning receiving the Royal Red Cross in recognition of her part in what had been achieved.

One of the most remarkable features of the war time period had been the way in which the ordinary work of the Infirmary continued. For five years, as more and more accommodation was allocated for military purposes, the admission and treatment, including many complex operations, of the sick of the district continued at a level not far from that of the pre-war period. Just as remarkable but less surprising given the previous experience, was the way in which the Infirmary's benefactors and the general public responded to the Managers' constant calls for financial support for this and that extension.

In January 1919 the military wards were closed and returned to the Infirmary for normal use. The Managers decided to retain the old cricket pavilion but to dispose of the last wooden extension which was sold for £145 and removed from the site. This left approximately seventy beds for civilian use, nearly forty more than in 1914, but it was soon evident that even this level of provision would be inadequate to meet the demand. The managers were allowed to keep the wartime

Gifts for the Soldiers.

Scottish Branch British Red Cross Society 3900 cigarettes and 25 lb. tobacco, 22nd July, 1916; 6000 cigarettes and 8 lb. tobacco, 20th October, 1916 ; 7000 cigarettes and 8 lb. tobacco, 23rd January, 1917; hamper of dressings on 4th July, 1916, 8th August, 30th September, 4th December, and 27th January, 1917; 6 or 8 dozen eggs weekly during April, May, July, August, and September, 1916; 10 dozen weekly during February and March, 1917 — in all during the year 160 dozen; 20 day shirts, 30 semmits, 30 pairs pants, 10 roller towels, 50 handkerchiefs, 20 pair slippers, 10 white bedcovers, 10 helmets, 10 mitts, 10 mufflers, stationery, soap, matches, and toothbrushes.

Red Cross Game Depot 1916 26th August, 5 brace grouse; 1917 22nd January, venison; 27th January, venison, 1 pheasant, 2 hares.

Mr. W. M. Cochran, George Town, British West Indies 2 boxes oranges.

The Convalescent Fund of the Soldiers' and Sailors' Association, Falkirk, per Mr. W. J. Gibson, Hon. Secretary: a quantity of cigarettes and tobacco.

Falkirk and District Tramways Co., per Mr. Hays—free passes on tramcars always to wounded soldiers and drive round the Ochil Hills (twice), also tea.

Bainsford Church Work Party 11 dozen eggs and 2 pots jam.

Polmont and District Work Centre, per Mrs. Gibson, 12 flannel binders.

Bainsford and Grahamston Co-operative Women's Guild 13 pairs bedroom slippers, 16s in money.

Carron Co-operative Women's Guild 30 pair socks, very large quantity of cakes, sweets, fruit, and jam (several times).

"Shell Girls" at Carron tea party for wounded soldiers in St. James Hall

"Munition Girls" of Falkirk Iron Co. large quantity of cigarettes and chocolates.

The Children of Irving Memorial Church, Camelon quantity of fruit, cakes, eggs, etc.

Ladies of Grangemouth, per Mr. Robertson large quantity of cigarettes (twice).

Ladies' Committee of Golf Club, Grangemouth £1 2s. 6d. to buy cigarettes, sweets, etc.

Grahamston Bowling Green Club tea party to wounded soldiers.

Larbert Parish Church Gift Service 12 dozen eggs, 24 boxes cigarettes, 1 tin biscuits, also fruit and vegetables, etc.

Falkirk Parish Church large basket of grapes.

Polmont U.F. Church Work Party — 12 pairs socks.

beds donated by the Marquis of Zetland as well as the material given throughout the war by the Red Cross and this certainly helped but the tide of demand seemed unstoppable.

Observers of the period have described communities like Falkirk as going 'hospital mad' as more and more people realised that the conditions from which they suffered were treatable, and treatable locally. The figures bear this out. In 1919 there were just under 400 'indoor' patients; by 1922 this had reached 637 and two years later a staggering 903. During the same period out-patients numbers rose from 500 to nearly 2,000 and operations almost doubled to 907. Frequently all beds were occupied and waiting lists of 30 or more were not uncommon. The cost of care was also rising — back in 1914 it had cost 3 shillings and nine pence per patient, per day but by 1920 it had risen to 6 shillings, an increase of nearly 70%. But long before then the Managers had read the signs and come to a momentous decision. In early 1920, perplexed by the rising tide of demand, they had called in the services of Colonel MacIntosh the Medical Superintendent of the Western Infirmary in Glasgow, and an eminent authority on questions of hospital construction.

> After examining the Infirmary and the ground available for extension and having in view the population and industrial character of the area which is served by it, he strongly recommended that money should not be spent on permanent extensions of the present Infirmary. He was of the opinion that the district would require a new Infirmary built on up-to-date lines on a site which would provide for a much larger Infirmary than could be erected on the present site.

Thus the Managers reported to the Annual General Meeting of subscribers on the 26th July, 1920. From then on only temporary measures would be taken at Thornhill Road, including the conversion of the pavilion into sleeping quarters for the nurses along with a small twelve bed ward. In July of the following year the subscribers approved a proposal to seek a new site and to establish a building and extension fund to raise the massive sums required.

It was a far cry from Mrs Gibson's little Cottage Hospital and sadly the old lady herself did not live to guide and inspire the planners. Her

death on 14th February 1919 just
after the end of the war robbed
the Managers of the kind of
enthusiasm and energy they
would need in abundance, but the
network of support she had
created over nearly four decades
proved a legacy more significant
than any buildings could ever be.
Soon afterwards her friends and
admirers on the Infirmary's
management committee decided
to honour her memory in a
tangible way. They launched an
appeal to raise the £300 required
to commission a marble bust of
the grand old lady from the
Glasgow sculptor Kellock Brown

and in 1921 this was installed in the Thornhill Road building as a
permanent tribute to their founder and lifelong support. In 1931 Mrs
Gibson's bust travelled with staff and patients to Gartcows and since
then has kept a watchful eye on the comings and goings in Falkirk
Infirmary from her vantage point on the central stairway. She will not
be moving to the Forth Valley Royal Hospital in Larbert but will remain
in the new Community Hospital at Gartcows, as a permanent reminder
of selfless service to health care in our community.

Back in post war Falkirk the Managers, bereft now of her inspiration,
faced the biggest challenge in the Infirmary's thirty year history. How
they went about answering it is the next part of this remarkable story.

CHAPTER FOUR

The Good Samaritans

The decade between the Managers' courageous decision to build a new Infirmary and the opening of the buildings for patients in 1931, was one of two interlinked stories. On the one hand we have the greatest fund-raising effort in the history of the district which filled the columns of the local newspapers and involved people of all ages and ranks in society. On the other, there is the day to day struggle in Thornhill Road to cope with a massive rise in demand in increasingly cramped and inadequate buildings on which the Managers had determined to spend as little as possible. Both stories are heroic, full of sacrifice and ingenuity and both crucial to the ultimate success of what was to follow.

As far as the decision to build new is concerned we may be sure that there were many who thought it was too grandiose an idea for a small town like Falkirk. Some argued that with large hospitals in Glasgow and Edinburgh just a train journey away Falkirk would be foolish to undertake such a costly project when the public would also have to find the huge sums every year thereafter to keep in running. The voluntary principle was a precious thing but only if it operated in the realms of the possible. In response the Managers pointed out the continuous increase in demand over the years and the numbers presently being turned away who were beginning to overload the city hospitals. As far as funding the future was concerned they pointed to the fact that since the war there had been a surplus of income each year of more than £2,000 and that they were losing subscriptions to Glasgow and Edinburgh because lack of beds at Thornhill Road. Undaunted by criticism and ever optimistic that the support would be there when required the Managers pressed on with the search for a suitable site for the new Infirmary and by the time they reported on progress to a public meeting in March 1922, the funds had already reached £8,439 and a year later had doubled to over £17,000. By then a suitable site had been found and the subscribers approved a proposal to pay £5,850 for:

> The purchase of a portion of the estate of Gartcows including the Mansion House, Offices, Policies and Home Parks, extending to approximately 11 acres which they were advised was an eminently suitable site for the purposes of an Infirmary from every standpoint.

From the outset they had decided to wait until they had raised £50,000 through the usual channels before launching a major public appeal for funds, and in April of 1924 they announced that the time was coming close:

> From accumulated money and bequests, the funds of the Infirmary in sight amount to approximately £50,000 and now that a site for the new Infirmary has been secured at Gartcows, it will be, in view of the ever increasing need for additional accommodation, be necessary for the Managers to exhaust every avenue in order to obtain the necessary funds to proceed with the new building scheme at the earliest possible moment, and they are at present considering the best means of attacking the problem. They earnestly solicit from the community not only a generous response to the appeal which will be made immediately but also their co-operation and assistance in promoting and carrying through special efforts to raise the large sum which is required.

A great public meeting was held the following year, on 27th April, 1925, in the Town Hall when over one thousand people from all over the district assembled to hear the campaign launched by the great and famous. The Marquis of Linlithgow and Colonel MacIntosh, along with the eminent surgeons Sir Norman Walker and Sir Henry Wade lent their considerable verbal weight to the call for support, and among the observers carried away on the tide of enthusiasm was the *Falkirk Herald*'s correspondent:

> An audience numbering fully one thousand representative of all classes of the people of East Stirlingshire assembled on Monday evening in Falkirk Town Hall to witness and assist in the launch of a ship which set sail on a mission surely more noble than any entered

upon in the past — for her destination is the great heart of the people. She is manned by a crew of three, Faith, Hope, and Charity. Faith in the nobility, no less than the necessity of her mission. Hope, blood brother of belief, in her triumphant return to harbour; and Charity, the steersman under whose guidance she will return home with hold brimful of treasure for the consummation of that mission. That the good ship Infirmary Appeal Campaign will accomplish her mission is the fervent desire of all whose life is illumined with a spark of humanity and that such was the feeling of the great meeting on Monday evening was amply evident.

The religious metaphor was appropriate, for the Good Samaritan became the symbol of the campaign for ever after, coupled with the motto dear to all Falkirk 'bairns' 'Touch ane, Touch a'. The publicity material which followed was less flowery and more hard hitting — stressing the grave position of the present Infirmary — the official appeal leaflet explained the reason for growth in demand and the need to build anew. Difficulties were underlined with potent examples of

The Marquis of Linlithgow addresses the rally on 27th April 1925

Architect W. J. Gibson's impression of the new infirmary 1925

inadequacy, 'X-ray department in a boxroom; eye clinic in the general office; pathologist without a laboratory; intolerable nurses quarters'. The leaflet concluded:

> The one thing with which no great community can dispense under modern conditions of life is an efficient infirmary . . . it is above all upon the multitude rather than the few that the success of this great cause depends. It is the cheerful self-sacrificing, enthusiastic liberality of all that alone can bring victory.

It was the prelude to an astonishing five year spell in which every conceivable method of fund-raising was employed, and hardly an organisation or individual failed to participate whether wittingly or not. If they attended a play or pantomime, part of the receipts went to the fund. The same applied to football matches and dances, school concerts and bus trips, picnics and whist drives. There were collecting boxes everywhere — outside hospital wards, in public buildings, in private houses, in shops and business premises. The appetite of the savers and collectors was further whetted when the first sketch plans of the proposed new Infirmary were made public by the architect who was, appropriately enough, W. J. Gibson, son of the Infirmary's founder herself who had masterminded the various wartime building projects at the Infirmary.   His plans showed just how ambitious and far-sighted the Managers had been — there would be 120 beds to start

W. J. Gibson pictured with his mother at Hatherley

with, with firm plans for an increase to over 200 as required. The artist's impression of the buildings and the plan published at the time show the wards branching out from a long central corridor with operating theatres, a large out-patient department and all the support services like catering, laundry, laboratories and pharmacy. Unlike Thornhill, it was hoped that there would be Maternity and Isolation Blocks and a place

A SUGGESTED PLAN OF THE PROPOSED NEW FALKIRK & DISTRICT INFIRMARY

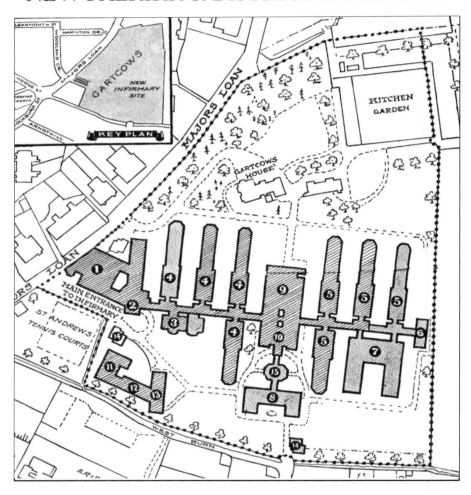

1. OUT-PATIENTS AND ORDINARY RECEPTION 2. CASUALTY RECEPTION
3. MAJOR OPERATING THEATRES 4. MEN'S WARD 5. WOMEN'S WARDS
6. ISOLATION BLOCK 7. CHILDREN'S AND MATERNITY BLOCK 8. NURSES'
HOME 9. KITCHEN, STORES, NURSES' AND SERVANT'S DINING HALLS,
ETC. 10. MATRON'S SISTERS' AND RESIDENT DOCTORS' QUARTERS,
SECRETARY, BOARD ROOM, ETC. 11. STEAM PLANT 12. WASH-HOUSE
13 LAUNDRY 14. GATE LODGES 15. HALL FOR SUN-BATH TREATMENT

was marked out for them on the plan though at this stage agreement on funding was still a matter of negotiation with the authorities. A nurses' home also appears as a future proposal and even 'a hall for sunburn treatment'. One further problem, unresolved at the time, was the position of the St Andrew's Tennis Club which occupied a key position on the Majors Loan end of the site. Its removal to another place was important to the project but the architect was not presumptuous enough to remove it from the plan at this stage.

The publicity gained from the publication of the drawings was immediate. They fired the imagination and the public responded. The target to be raised was £120,000, an astonishing amount, which equates to around £3 million in today's terms, and this in an era when there was neither lottery, nor European Funding and precious little in the form of Government subsidy.

The overwhelming impression which comes through from newspaper articles and official reports, concert programmes and souvenirs is of a great and happy collaboration of all the people of the district in securing 'their' Infirmary. Every square yard of the site, every brick of the buildings, every stick of furniture and equipment and every penny of wages and salaries would be provided by the people. 'Touch ane, Touch a' proclaimed the motto, and the response was the most eloquent proof of the truth of its message.

A glance through the local newspapers for 1926 and '27 reveals a frenzy of fund-raising activity. One might for example, enjoy 'The Merchant of Venice' at the Dobbie Hall, 'Floradora' in the Grand Theatre, or 'She Stoops to Conquer' in the Town Hall. There was a 'Fancy Fair' and '6d. bazaar' in the YMCA hut, 'Mr Martin's Orchestra Dance' in the Gymnasium, Camelon, 'Music in the Garden' at Arnothill, a 'Vocal Recital' in the Masonic Temple and a 'Palais de Danse' in the Temperance Cafe. For sporting types there were football, cricket and tennis competitions as well as the chance to see a 'Great Boxing Gala in Jim Paterson's new and commodious Pavilion' to see 'a four round contest between Spowart's midgets' along with Falkirk's own 'Fatty Wells, Young Connell and Butcher Anderson'.

There were road races, grand penny trails, watch-winding competitions, highland gatherings, popular lectures, community singing, open days at mansion houses, jumble sales and silver paper

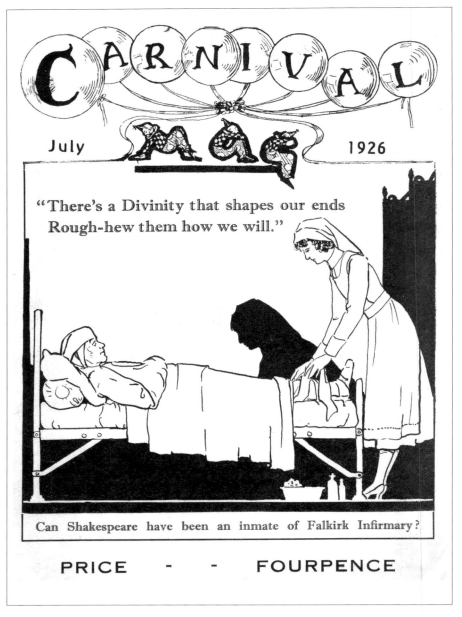

Student's Rag Magazine from 1926

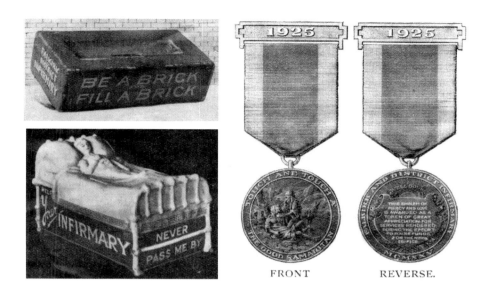

FRONT   REVERSE.

Collecting Boxes and Medals

collections. There were official 'Infirmary Weeks' with great carnivals of students in fancy dress and decorated floats parading through the streets of the town. The list was endless. Indeed the full-time appeal organiser Mr H. Crowe and his fund-raising Committee in their Kirk Wynd office, left no possible avenue unexplored in pursuit of the illusive bawbees. A small book was produced entitled 'Seventy Three Ways in Which You Can Help YourInfirmary' and it included as number 32:

> Strap onto your dog a collecting box and teach him to make collections but not in public thoroughfares without a special permit.

Number 45 was even more daunting:

> Carry an Infirmary Collecting Box when you are travelling by train or tram or going a long journey, and put the claims of the Infirmary before follow passengers in a quiet, interesting manner.

For those collectors who raised a guinea or more a special medal was available decorated with coloured ribbon and the Good Samaritan with the message:

EAST STIRLINGSHIRE

THE WELFARE OF ONE AND ALL IN *East Stirlingshire* IS DEPENDANT UPON THE ADEQUACY AND EFFICIENCY OF THE FALKIRK & DISTRICT INFIRMARY

MOVED BY THE SPIRIT OF THE ANCIENT WATCHWORD
" *Touch ane touch a'* "
LET US STAND SHOULDER TO SHOULDER IN SUPPORT
of
THE TASK BEFORE US

BETTER MEDDLE WITH DISEASE THAN LET DISEASE MEDDLE WITH EAST STIRLINGSHIRE

Fundraising advertisements from the 1920s

This emblem of mercy and love is awarded as a token of great appreciation for services rendered during the effort to raise funds for the new edifice.

The collecting boxes themselves were novel — one shaped like a brick exhorted 'Be a Brick — fill a Brick', while the other showed a patient in bed with the message 'Never Pass Me By'. Sufficient bricks were filled and the boxes seldom passed by, and, at the end of 1925, over £75,000 had been raised.

By the time the Duchess of Montrose cut the first sod at Gartcows in a downpour on 10th November, 1926 the fund had reached nearly £90,000, well within sight of the target. The large crowd which gathered on the open site heard the Duke of Montrose and Charles W Forbes of Callendar sing the praises of the 'voluntary principle,' which they said inspired such mighty co-operation among people of all ranks. After the ceremony the official party toured the Infirmary in Thornhill Road before retiring to Callendar House for afternoon tea! From that day on work continued apace and soon the public could see in bricks and mortar the buildings which they had laboured so hard to provide.

It is interesting to compare the fund-raising campaigns of the 1880s and 90s with the events of the 1920s. In the first case the money came in the main from the well-heeled middle classes whose consciences

Cutting of the first sod of earth at Gartcows in November 1926

Pram-pushing students raise money in Grangemouth in 1926

prompted them to do what they saw as their Christian duty to the poorest and weakest in society. Now, in a new post war world, it was the ordinary men, women and children themselves who undertook the bulk of the fund raising albeit with the support and leadership of the influential members of the management committee still dominated by successful men of business. It was, as Forbes of Callendar had said, a powerful combination which was to serve the community well for the next thirty years during which time, of course, the dream of a magnificent new Infirmary was fulfilled.

Grangemouth supports the Infirmary Appeal

Miss Yule and her nursing and domestic staff in the early 1920s

In the meantime, while the razzmatazz of campaign and collection went on, the work of caring for the sick and injured of the district continued as before. Always stretched for ward space and vital ancillary accommodation, the growing number of nurses struggled to maintain the high standards of care which Matrons Joss and Glendinning had established. In February, 1920 after over 19 years service Miss Hannah Glendinning asked the Managers' agreement to retire and this was accepted with much regret. To mark her departure Miss Glendinning was presented with an honorarium of £400 and a silver salver in appreciation of her efforts, particularly during the war when she had sustained the Infirmary despite tremendous difficulties. It is a measure of the importance of the post that sixty qualified and experienced nursing sisters from throughout Scotland applied for her job, and from them the Managers chose Miss Susan McIntosh from Edinburgh, a Sister with considerable hospital experience at home and overseas.

In the same year the Managers resolved to rename the Infirmary to reflect the much wider area and larger population served — now it was to be Falkirk *and District* Infirmary. After the relatively short period of three years Miss McIntosh left to take up an appointment as Matron of Dundee Royal Infirmary, and she was replaced in February, 1923 by Miss Margaret Arnott Yule from Paisley, who like her predecessor had seen service abroad during the war. The following year two distingished honorary consultants to the Infirmary were appointed namely Mr (later Sir) Henry Wade, a Falkirk man who was surgeon in Edinburgh Royal Infirmary, and Mr (later Sir) David Wilkie, Professor of Surgery at Edinburgh University. At the same time the regular services of Pathologist Dr W J Logie were also secured. These appointments were proof if any was needed that the Managers were determined to continue and develop the quality of service to the patients of the district despite the severe difficulties faced at the steadily deteriorating site.

The numbers of patients continued to rise dramatically — by 1928 there were over 1,000 in-patients for the first time ever with over 4,000 out-patients, almost eight times the number catered for in the last year of the war. In addition there were 2,172 operations, a quarter involving major surgery. As early as 1923 the Infirmary had opened a well equipped Ophthalmic Department under the direction of Dr J.

Falkirk Infirmary in the 1920s

The Ward Kitchen

The Nurses Common Room and Bedroom

The Infirmary Larder

The back of the Infirmary with the wooden hut to the right

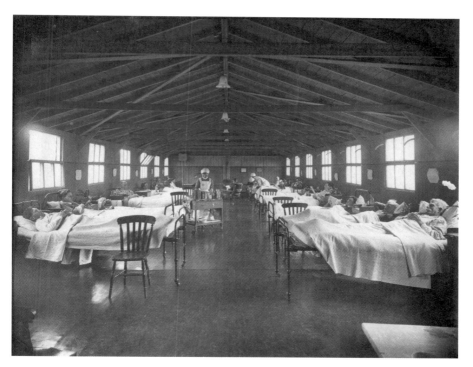

The male ward

Pendleton-White, and in 1926 an additional out-patients department, namely Ear, Nose and Throat, was established under the charge of Dr G. B. Brand of Glasgow. During that year over 1,100 patients attended for E.N.T. treatment with Ophthalmics assisting nearly 900.

Despite the concentration on fund-raising for the new Infirmary the 'normal' collections and employee contributions provided sufficient funds to sustain the service at Thornhill Road and, in several years, pass on a surplus to the Appeal Fund. It is interesting to note that the urgent need to raise funds did not change in any way the principles of the institution enshrined in the regular statement that 'non-subscribers are expected to pay for treatment in accordance with their means but no one is refused admission on account of inability to contribute'. And this fully two decades before the birth of the National Health Service.

The Managers' Report for the year 1922 contains one very interesting comment which signalled yet another major step in the

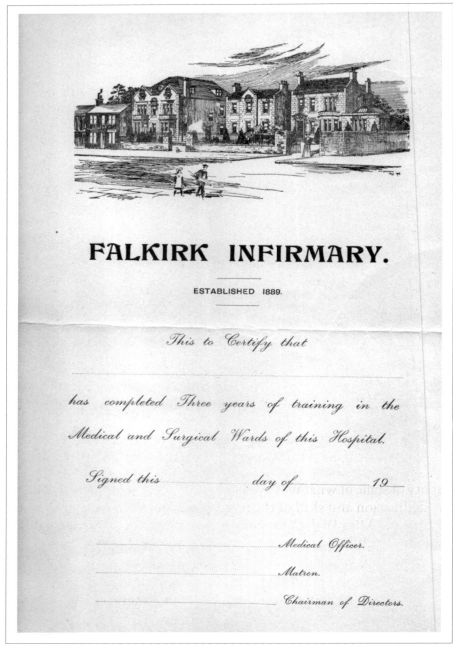

Nurses Certificate before 1922

forward progress of Falkirk and District Infirmary:

> The GeneralNursing Council have granted provisional recognition of the Infirmary as a training centre for nurses. To assist probationers in their studies and coach them for the examinations arranged by the Nursing Council, the Managers have engaged the services of a visiting Sister tutor who revises the work done in the Institution and supplements where necessary.

From its very earliest days the Infirmary had recruited nurses as probationers and, after a three year training period, they were considered qualified if the Medical Officer and Matron judged that they had achieved an acceptable standard. The certificate printed on the opposite page was all that was required. After 1922 Falkirk probationers seeking registration with the General Council had to take formal examinations in Edinburgh after studying and attending lectures in their off-duty hours. From time to time the Annual Reports in the 1920s thank individual doctors for providing lectures, among them Dr Harper of Grangemouth and Dr W J Logie, whose long connection with the Infirmary will be mentioned later in this account.

Many people in the district still remember the old Infirmary in these final years and some have passed on their memories which in the main support the descriptions we have of a happy and successful institution battling against shortage of space and equipment. One commented on the 'almost ceaseless activity with the resources of the Infirmary taxed to the utmost'. Miss Susan Baird of Maddiston joined the nursing staff in the 1920s from a much newer hospital in the West of Scotland. She was surprised at the shortage of materials and at the quality of some of what was available though she soon came to admire the dedication and skill of the medical and nursing staff. Indeed Dr Hunter and Miss Dick the senior sister are repeatedly singled out as the outstanding personalities in the daily life of the Infirmary impressing all who came into contact with them. One former Sister remembered well:

> Our Chief was Dr A E Hunter who was on-call at all hours. He was always so helpful and dignified and really was worshipped by all.

One patient remembered the Matron Miss Yule as 'a real dragon'

Miss Dick (right) with the Operating Theatre staff in the late 1920s

after receiving the sharp end of her tongue over an untidy locker and another recalled being taken to the Infirmary to have an operation to remove a nose blockage. He joined a queue of other small boys and left four hours later with his tonsils removed! Many described the high number of tonsil operations conducted in those days and the strain this put on resources. Dr 'Daddy' Brand the ENT specialist had developed a special technique in which the child was anaesthetised whilst sitting upright on a nurse's knee and the operation conducted with the nurse supporting the child's head. Miss Baird recalls seeing little white-faced children resting four to a bed, two at each end, covered to the chin with a red waterproof sheet. There they recovered for a couple of hours before their parents returned to collect them. Sometimes the treatment offered to out-patients was more out of the ordinary. One man recalls his father in the years after the first World War and still suffering from rheumatism:

> He was told to report to the old Infirmary for treatment for rheumatism. This consisted of electric shocks from batteries enclosed within a wooden box. Two lengths of flex with handgrips were placed in patients hands while a nurse turned a handle at the side of the box. He had this treatment for sometime — I think it helped him a lot.

In October of 1928 the new Infirmary appeal was brought to an end by a 'Grand Bazaar' opened by the Secretary of State for Scotland Sir John Gilmour, which would, it was hoped raise the final £5,000 required. For three days great crowds flocked to the Drill Hall where stall holders from all over the district sold their wares. When the last penny was counted the astonishing total raised was £9,600, the largest sum ever achieved by bazaar in a Scottish provincial town. Today's equivalent figure would be close to £200,000! By the end of 1930 the new building was ready for inspection and in two weeks in December nearly 8000 visitors did just that. The Publicity Committee did not miss the opportunity — 'Your Infirmary — You've Seen It! What about it?' declared the leaflet issued to the visitors. 'Aye, it's up alright, but how is it going to be kept up?' The staff would need to double and the money had to come from somewhere. Once again the appeal to all the people was made with complete confidence.

Shortly before the new building was completed the Matron Miss Yule retired and her assistant, Sister Anna C Dick, was given the task of leading the greatly increased nursing staff to their splendid new home in Gartcows. In February 1931 the patients were removed over one weekend from Thornhill Road and the old building which had served for so long was left to find a new role. It was the end of an era and the beginning of a new and illustrious chapter in the history of hospital care in Falkirk district.

"TOUCH ANE, TOUCH A'."

ALL in the wide area of East Stirlingshire. served by the Infirmary, are familiar with the ancient watchword of the Burgh in which their activities are centred. We are proud to recall that Historians claim for our community "a reputation for pugnacity and for standing by one another in a difficulty which is enjoyed to the same extent by none other in Scotland."

Let us to-day revitalise the old watchword and re-claim the old repute; adopting them for a wider area and infusing into them the noblest, most generous and humane spirit.

"Touch ane, touch a'" runs the brave legend. It is not man's touch we fear to-day. the human invader we would stand shoulder to shoulder to repel; but the touch of disease and infection, the de'il of cruel accident that inflicts pain and suffering, maims the limb and tortures the mind.

The suffering and sickness of one touch all; all must rally to the support of the ill and distressed. It is surely no more than common sense, even at the bidding of our own interests and well-being. to see to it that we give the most strenuous and hearty support to the provision and maintenance of a worthy and efficiently equipped Infirmary for East Stirlingshire to maintain our vigour and health.

"Better meddle wi' disease than let disease meddle wi' the bairns of East Stirlingshire."

Infirmary Appeal Poster from 1926

CHAPTER FIVE

A Triumph of Co-operation

For Miss Dick and her staff the new buildings offered, at long last, the opportunity to provide for all the medical needs of the people of the district. The Maternity and Isolation units financed by the Local Authority added a new dimension to the work of the Infirmary, and the surgical facilities were on a par with the finest in the country. But it was space, so much space everywhere, which made the Gartcows site such a transformation from the cramped Thornhill quarters hemmed in as they were by town housing. In 1931 the new Infirmary lay outside the town in what were still relatively wide open spaces; whatever demands the future might bring there was land in abundance and the Managers inspired choice of site would prove their shrewdest and most far reaching decision. The design of the building was also inventive with the five 18 bed wards branching out from the main, 500 foot long, central corridor to the south so that they had light on three sides. With the addition of sun wards and private side wards this provided a grand total of 26 beds in each. Each ward had one central fireplace which heated air which was then circulated through the ward via conduits in the floor. Verandahs were attached to each ward to provide fresh air sleeping conditions when the weather allowed! On the opposite side of the corridor were two major operating theatres only one of which was equipped at the outset.

The plans published back in 1925 had been modified to reflect successful negotiations with the St Andrew's Tennis Club which moved away from Majors Loan allowing the completion of the main entrance and the relocation of the Isolation Block from its original planned position at the far end of the site. This building for the treatment of 'skin and other infectious diseases' — particularly the unmentionable 'gentlemen's social diseases' — was one of two sections which was not wholly funded by the normal voluntary methods but

was in part paid for by the local health authorities. The same was true of the Maternity Wards which were located on the north side of the main corridor at the far end from the main entrance. Here there was a two ward unit with ancillary accommodation providing 24 beds. In praising the facilites here, *The Scottish Nurse* magazine for March 1931 reported that

> The windows of the larder here and elsewhere are fitted with a special glass of yellow tint, which does not attract flies. The bathing apparatus is particularly up-to-date, each bath being constructed on wheels, with a brake for locking the bath at any angle.

There was of course a major out-patients department near the main entrance with a large central waiting room with accommodation for 250 people as well as consulting rooms and, arranged close by, the ENT, ophthalmic and casualty departments. Here too there were two minor operating theatres and recovery rooms as well as the X-ray department with the most up-to-date apparatus available. Over £1,000 was spent on surgical instruments and apparatus and there was a 'specially constructed X-ray photograph recess with glass front'. This meant that:

By placing the photograph within this recess and switching on a light behind, the surgeon may have a complete shadow of his subject in his constant view while operating.

In the centre of the main corridor on the south side, the architect had set the Memorial Hall, now long since disappeared. Described at the time as 'one of the outstanding architectural features of the Infirmary' it had walls lined with fine wood panelling and all the handsome endowment boards from the old Infirmary. The bust of Mrs Gibson was also located in a specially alcove and there was a 'double dial clock which is electrically controlled'. On the south side of the wall was a beautiful stained glass window of the Good Samaritan, the symbol of the Infirmary.

The outside of the buildings were equally impressive. The main entrance to the Infirmary from Major's Loan had fine wrought iron gates provided by former pupils of Falkirk High School in memory of their colleagues who had fallen in the great war. Decorative railings, pillared walls, a rock garden and dear old Jenny Mair's Burn which had run through the estate since time immemorial, formed 'sparkling cascades and pools' with a large lily pond and a carved stone fountain.

Beyond the gates was a decorative arch bearing the coat of arms of Falkirk and on the other side the entrance for emergency vehicles close to the main corridor and the operating theatres. To the left of the arch stood the building which has become over the decades the symbol of Falkirk and District Royal Infirmary, the administrative block which bears the clock, royal arms and the name of the institution. This building provided space for six doctors, the matron's quarters, the board room, the out-patients department already described, the in-patients reception and other office accommodation. The road which is now called Westburn Avenue was newly made in 1931 and referred to then as 'the New Road'. Between the road and the building 'broad lawns form a bright green carpet broken here and there by some fine trees happily saved from those which adorned the estate.' The two storey building on the opposite side of the corridor from the Memorial Hall housed the nurses dining and recreation halls and its handsome facade bore the carved, linked coats-of-arms of Falkirk, Denny, Grangemouth and of Stirling County.

The dining and recreation hall building facing Westburn Avenue

The coat-of-arms on the pediment of the building opposite.
Falkirk (centre), Grangemouth (left), Denny (right)
and the County of Stirling County (top)

In the early months 85 beds were brought into service in three wards, for children and male and female medical/surgical. The number of nursing and domestic staff, still called maids, was increased to cope with the new demands and at the end of the year Miss Dick had 8 sisters, 37 nurses and 20 maids. One thing that was missing was adequate accommodation for this large group who were expected to live on the premises. That would have to wait on a new wave of fundraising and in the meantime the old mansion house of Gartcows, the creaking, ivy-covered home of generations of Heughs, was converted to provide rooms for the staff. It stood in the grounds to the west of the wards and even with its days of elegance fast fading it was a marked improvement on the partitioned living quarters in the old wooden hut at Thornhill. Nonetheless it was still far from adequate and the provision of a proper nurses home as envisaged by the architect became the major concern of the Managers for the next two decades or more.

In the meantime Infirmary President Dr John Young and the Managers had two more immediate problems. The first was, as ever, financial. The new Infirmary with increased provision meant additional staffing and running costs and once again the Managers turned to the public for help. Enlisting the assistance of the new Secretary of State

The in-patients and out-patients departments

The Bonnybridge Band greets the Prince

for Scotland William Adamson, they held yet another open meeting at which it was 'unanimously agreed to increase the employees subscriptions from one penny per week to twopence per week and the individual subscription to ten shillings'. The result was a fifty per cent increase in income during 1931 and, even though that years expenditure jumped by a massive seventy per cent, the books were still balanced and a small surplus applied to the building fund.

The second problem was more pleasant. No official opening ceremony was held in 1931 while the Managers worked behind the scenes to secure the attendance of a royal visitor. They were successful and at the end of the year it was announced that the Infirmary would be opened by HRH Prince George, third son of King George V and future Duke of Kent, on Monday, 11th January, 1932 during a visit to the town. A huge logistical exercise was undertaken to ensure that all went smoothly on the day but to the consternation of everyone involved the Prince was unwell and called off at a late stage throwing the whole exercise into confusion. One can hardly imagine the panic as all the prepared plans had to be rearranged involving hundreds of guests,

policing, bands, schools etc but a simple move forward one week solved the problem and all was well.

To an age in which the majority are fairly indifferent to royal visits it is difficult to convey adequately the enthusiasm which greeted this news. In the *Falkirk Herald* it was described as a 'lustrous page' in the town's 'long and honourable history'. Certainly 'The Day' as it was described brought huge crowds to the streets with shops, offices, schools and factories closing early to allow as many as possible to attend. In the event over 20,000 people stood for hours in blustery January weather to greet the Prince, who visited Carron Company before driving to the Infirmary in the afternoon. Most of the streets in the vicinity of Majors Loan and Cockburn Street were closed and several stands and enclosures were erected for invited guests. The uniformed organisations of the district formed a guard of honour in the streets and nursing staff lined the main corridors of the Infirmary. The Pathe News cameras were rolling as the Prince and his entourage were greeted by the Lord Lieutenant of the County of Stirling, and the Bonnybridge and District Band played the National Anthem. After Psalm 100 and a prayer of dedication from the Rev J A Dean of Erskine

Church, Prince George was officially welcomed by Dr Young on behalf of the Managers and subscribers. After apologising for the cancellation of the original date, he declared the new Infirmary to be a 'triumph of co-operation' and told the gathered crowds that:

> His Majesty has been graciously pleased to grant the inclusion of the title 'Royal' in the name of the Institution and to direct accordingly that the Institution should in future be designated The Falkirk and District Royal Infirmary

This announcement was greeted by rapturous applause from the spectators though, of course, the news came as no great surprise. After all the building was already emblazoned with the inscription FALKIRK AND DISTRICT . . . . . INFIRMARY, and it did not take a genius to fill in the space! After the rest of the Prince's short speech the party moved to the Memorial Hall where leading members of the medical staff, management and community were presented to Prince George who completed all the usual ceremonies which characterised such occasions — a bronze tablet was unveiled, a gold plated trowel presented, historical records deposited in a stone, and a blackthorn tree planted in the grounds. After tea the Prince toured the Infirmary and spoke to staff and patients throughout the building. By half-past three 'The Day' was over and the entourage departed leaving a happy

and satisfied crowd many of whom, even at this distance in time recall the occasion with pride, not only because a famous face was in attendance but because it celebrated the successful conclusion of the greatest community fund raising effort the district has ever seen either before or since. More than £120,000 was raised — nearly £3 million in today's terms — and the Infirmary opened entirely free of debt.

The Matron with the nursing staff in 1932

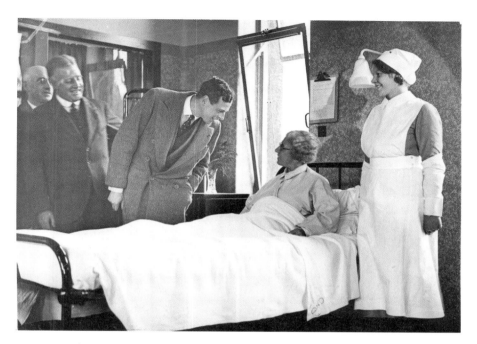

Over the years which followed the Infirmary continued to grow towards the size envisaged by the Managers and allowed for by the architect. By 1933 in-patient numbers were in excess of 2,000 with over 5,000 out-patients and the Matron had 9 sisters and 54 nurses. By then the planned figure of 120 beds had been passed and three years later the long-term target of 200 was reached. In-patients exceeded 2,700 and out-patients 6,000 and over 4,000 operations were carried out. There were now 10 sisters, 63 nurses and and assistant Matron working under Miss Dick and on the medical side the Infirmary had four resident physicians and a very large number of visiting consultants — surgeons in a variety of specialisms, as well as radiologists and oto-laryngologists, obstetricians, gynaecologists, pathologists, anaesthetists, dental surgeons and dermatologists. In 1936, seven wards were in use — female medical and surgical, male medical and surgical, male orthopaedic, a new childrens' ward which opened in 1935, and the maternity ward with 25 beds and 2 labour rooms. Specialist equipment like the 'giant magnet' in ophthalmics, the 'Manlove steam steriliser' and the 'swivel baths, the first of their kind to be installed in the country' already mentioned helped reinforce

The medical staff in 1932

the idea that Falkirk and District Royal Infirmary was an up-to-date, well equipped and progressive institution on a par with the best in the country.

But the task of keeping it there was increasingly difficult and the Managers waged a constant battle to maintain the required level of support from the people of the district. In 1933 for the first time for many years income failed to cover outgoings, and thereafter special Christmas Appeals to make good the shortfalls became commonplace. Despite this setback the Managers reaffirmed their faith in the Infirmary's future by purchasing an extra eleven acres of land lying to the west of the buildings from the Aitken family in the same year. There were many new calls on the scarce resources as medical knowledge advanced and new treatments emerged. Even before the move to Gartcows a special fund had been set up to finance the purchase of £700 worth of Radium — 'the minimum quantity which would have a curative value' — and thus avoid, 'borrowing from another Institution for a limited period'.

Throughout the district fund raising continued as before with annual student street carnivals as the main feature. Assistance in kind as well as cash continued much as it had before, and one interesting donation in 1936 came from the Outram Press Wireless Fund which installed 136 earphones and 10 loudspeakers throughout the Infirmary. One of the most active of the support groups was the ladies 'Linen Guild' which had been founded in 1929. As well as paying an annual subscription to the Guild, lady members pledged to make or supply at least two articles from a prescribed list, which included nightshirts of 'unbleached twilled calico', gowns of 'grey union flannel', nightshirts of 'pink winceyette' and sheets, theatre gowns and pillowcases. Each year between two and three thousand such articles were handed over to the Infirmary reinforcing once again the idea that the people of the district and their Infirmary were bound together in a common purpose. The Managers were at pains to keep the Infirmary in the forefront of peoples' minds and to sustain this idea of the Infirmary as the joint responsibility of all the people, and while the sheer scale of the operation and the level of finance involved was beginning to strain the voluntary principle, most still believed that the co-operative spirit which had brought them thus far would survive. One example of the

The Board of Management of Falkirk and District Royal Infirmary in 1932

Front : Provost J Burnett White, Provost A. G. Logan, Rev. J. A. F. Dean, Thomas Thornley, Dr John Young, Fred Johnston, George Pate, Mr H. B. Watson, Alex Calender. Middle: Miss A. Gray-Buchanan, Dr D. C. Maclachlan, Mrs Murray, Mr W. R. Aitken, Duncan Kennedy, Miss O. A. Hume, James Fairlie, Mrs W. J. Gibson, Mrs Waugh, George McLaren. Back: James Prentice, Mrs Rennie, Mr J. M. Donald, Mrs Wilkie, Daniel Robertson, Robert Anderson, William Walker, Andrew Graham.

kind of publicity secured by the Managers was a series of articles in the *Falkirk Herald* in which 'Mr Everyman' visited a particular department asking questions and receiving detailed answers from the duty sisters and doctors which helped explain how important their work was to the people of the district. In one of the first of these the Matron, Miss Dick, conducted Mr Everyman round the wards:

> MR EVERYMAN Thank you for showing me round the Wards Matron. I did not realise until now what a vast amount of terrible pain and serious disease, men and women actually have to endure.

> MATRON Very few people outside the Infirmary have any clear conception of that Mr Everyman. In every hospital someone's life is hanging by a thread every hour of every day. It is the business of the doctors and the nurses, so far as is humanly possible to do so, to prevent that frail thread of life from snapping.

In the lengthy article which followed the Matron returns several times to the shortage of accommodation for her nurses which was, of course, the problem which exercised the Managers' minds most often in the 1930s. The rapid increase in numbers as new wards were completed led to the addition of a double ward in 1935 to serve as

The Mansion house of Gartcows

temporary accommodation, and then to a decision to build a new nurses' home as originally proposed by the architect. They once again turned to the public to appeal for the £40,000 required to provide proper facilities for present, as well as possible future staff requirements. The employees of the district were persuaded to accept a subscription increase from twopence to threepence a week of which one penny would go to the fund. Individual subscriptions were increased to thirteen shillings per annum with three shillings going to support the appeal. By the time the campaign was launched officially in 1937 over £10,000 had been subscribed. The large audience which filled the Town Hall in April that year

Sums promised or received . £12,700
Balance still required . £27,300

NURSES' GARDEN FETE
in the Grounds
of the Royal Infirmary
SATURDAY, 19th JUNE

heard from Sir George Stirling of Glorat, the Lord Lieutenant, and from Colonel Alan Stein, Chairman of the Infirmary as well as from two local MPs, that the lack of proper accommodation for staff was

holding up the expansion of patient care and creating long waiting lists. Extra beds were being placed along the middle of each ward in an effort to relieve the pressure, but vital ward space was still being used for the nurses and only by releasing this could the Infirmary answer all the calls now being made on its services. Apart from that, the community owed a debt of honour to the hard working

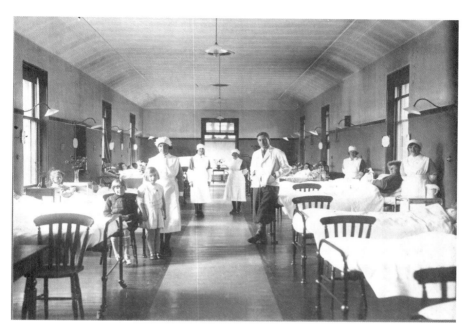

Doctor in plus fours visits the female ward.

Ward 3 Female Surgical

staff on whom so much depended. Once more a frantic round of fundraising gripped the district and the local newspapers were again filled with reports of dances and fetes, football matches, exhibitions and concerts. The nurses held a successful garden fete in June and by the end of the year half of the total was secured.

In March 1938, two new houses in Gartcows Drive were purchased to help alleviate the situation and allow for some expansion in staffing. A year later, with over £30,000 already gathered, the proposed plans of the nurses home were published, showing a three to five storey building with extensive bedroom accommodation for nursing and domestic staff. The push to collect the final funds continued with even more enthusiasm.

In the meantime the Managers fought to balance the books with ever increasing expenditure always threatening to run away from the income voluntarily subscribed by the public. That they were successful in every year except two in the first fifty years of existence, is a tribute to their skill and energy but the task was getting more difficult each year. In 1937 the Managers reported their biggest ever annual income figure of £23,900 but this was nearly matched by outgoings of £23,800 also the biggest ever. The patient statistics were staggering: in-patients 2807, out-patients 6074 making over 36,000 attendances, over 1000 major operations and 444 babies born. The average stay in hospital was 21 days and the number of beds in daily occupation 164. Long serving Treasurer James Allan voiced his concerns and did not confine his observations to financial affairs. There were, he thought, far too many operations on juveniles, with, for example, 500 children still waiting to have their tonsils and adenoids removed:

> This should be carefully gone into. They did not require to have bits chopped off them in older days to fit them for life.

Predictably the Medical Superintendent Dr John Young did not agree but they certainly agreed about a second point. There were far too many admissions as a result of injuries at work and from cuts etc being ignored at the time leading to septicaemia. There was a need for proper training, safer working conditions and adequate on-site first aid services. These would help prevent the overloading of the hard pressed Infirmary staff. It was an interesting early example of the emphasis on prevention rather than cure which would come to dominate medical thinking in the years ahead.

The following year, 1938 brought a significant deficit of £2,835 and Colonel Stein suggested that voluntary hospitals ought to be receiving state support since they provided many services to non-subscribing patients. They ought to be treated like the universities since they spent a great deal of time and resources in training doctors and nurses for the general benefit of the nation. This would help institutions like Falkirk and District Royal Infirmary to cope with ever increasing costs of vital supplies and equipment, as well as to improve staff conditions by increasing wages and reducing hours in line with national trends. And to underline their commitment to such training the Managers opened new Demonstration Rooms for nurses in training at a cost of £560. Pending such external financial support, the Managers hoped to wipe out the deficit by even more energetic fundraising. Fortunately they had just the peg on which to hang a new appeal in the shape of 'Infirmary Week' — a celebration of the Infirmary's 50th Anniversary in September 1939. Elaborate plans were drawn up including, dances, sports events, concerts, whist drives and other entertainments but in the end only a flag day and the publication of an historical booklet survived, for September 1939 brought the

Student fund-raisers in costume

The wartime huts built in 1939 and still in use today

declaration of war with Germany and the subsequent abandonment of most of the programme. Despite the likely increased demands for ward space the Managers accepted the advice of the Board of Health and delayed the erection of the nurses' home until after the war. A grant of £350 was received to help blackout the buildings and £375 to allow the construction of air-raid shelters in the grounds. Once again the Managers and their hard-pressed staff prepared themselves to answer national as well local needs.

Six months before the German invasion of Poland plunged Europe into war for the second time in a generation, the Board of Health had identified Falkirk and District Royal Infirmary as one of twelve centres in Scotland for the emergency treatment of air-raid casualties. In one of their earliest comments on the Infirmary's war time role the Managers summed up the prevailing view as follows:

> It was generally accepted that immediately following upon declaration of war this country would be subjected to intensive air-raids on a large scale which would involve a great many casualties among the civilian population.

To cope with such a disaster in the central area the Board proposed to erect nine wooden huts on vacant land close to the wards which would provide around three hundred extra places. In addition sixty of the hospital's existing beds would be reserved for military or civilian casualties arising from the hostilities. Predictably the Managers pledged total support for the war effort and September saw the evacuation of all convalescent patients to their own homes and a start made on a whole range of air-raid precautions. Within a few weeks blackouts were constructed for ward windows, black paint applied liberally, sandbags brought in and brick screens erected to protect wards and operating theatres from blast. Although the predicted air-raids did not materialise the preparations went on into early 1940 by which time over one hundred VAD auxiliary nurses had been trained in the work of the hospital and appeals were made in the local press for stretcher bearers and for billets for the extra medical staff. Female medical patients were transferred to one of the wooden huts from Ward 2 which had its windows bricked up and was equipped as a Resuscitation Ward on stand-by to give immediate treatment to fire and blast victims.

But it was not enemy bombing that brought the first casualties to Falkirk. In June 1940 over 300,000 soldiers were evacuated from Dunkirk and the wounded were dispersed to the waiting hospitals throughout the kingdom. For the staff in Falkirk Royal it was the

Patriotic nurses in a 1940 infirmary concert

moment they had been preparing for yet dreading:

> The first convoy of wounded soldiers arrived at Larbert Station —
> they had been in transit for three days, wounded at Dunkirk. This
> was a very harrowing experience for young nurses who had never
> seen such suffering before. Dr Hunter and Mr Tennent came and
> the operations began — the Sisters were hardly off-duty.

Two of the huts were occupied by soldiers from the Kings Own
Scottish Borderers and the Officer in Charge was Major Bannerman
who insisted on normal regimental routines on his daily visits to the
Infirmary. Although mercifully the predicted air-raid casualties did
not materialise on the scale imagined before the war the staff did care
for many wounded soldiers as well as German prisoners-of-war and
evacuees from England and even farther afield. One sister remembers
the German soldiers in one of the huts, terribly wounded but,
predictably 'some mother's laddies' in need of, and receiving, the same
care and attention as the other patients. Then there was the group of
very elderly Jewish women from Latvia and Czechoslovakia moved north
from Coventry and London during the blitz after escaping from war
torn Europe. They are remembered as frightened and confused as well
as ill, and speaking little or no English.

In October 1940 a new organisation was formed called 'The Falkirk
and District Royal Infirmary Samaritan Society' with the aim of
providing aftercare services and help for patients, military and civilian,
during convalescence. During the war too the general work of the
Infirmary continued and new departments of urology and orthopaedics
were opened. And to honour the continuing service of their physician
a bed in Ward 4 was named the 'Andrew E Hunter Bed' in March
1942.

One wartime incident which was kept quiet involved the first civil
use of penicillin in the Infirmary. In August 1943 permission was
granted by the War Office for Major Bannerman to collect sufficient
of the antibiotic — £100 worth — for one treatment, and this was
administered by Dr William Bell at 9 pm one evening with all medical
staff and a number of other associates of the hospital present.

A second incident kept even quieter at the time — and for a long
time afterwards — involved the treatment of a member of the ground

The Infirmary kitchen

crew at Grangemouth Aerodrome. The RAF had a number of Lysander aircraft based there with the capacity, if required, to spray poison gas which was, of course, stored at Grangemouth. The intention was that it would only be used if the enemy used it first. In the process of moving a cylinder of mustard gas a man received serious burns and was taken immediately under conditions of great secrecy to the Infirmary for treatment. And as far as the world outside was concerned it didn't happen at all!

The total number of patients treated continued to rise during the war years with around 3,000 in-patients in 1939 rising to 4,000 in 1945. At the same time the number of out-patient visits rose by 10,000 to nearly 40,000 during the last year of the war. Nursing staff increased from 79 to 96 supplemented of course by the VAD auxiliaries. It was a world of blackouts, tin hats and gas masks; of ration books, clothing coupons and identity cards; of dried eggs and powdered milk; of constant shortages, of make and mend, of use and wash and use again. Wards were often crowded with fold-up army camp beds set between hospital beds and working hours were long, time-off short and nurses

The new Board of Management after nationalisation

accommodation even worse than before the war.

In 1945 with the war in Europe over, conditions were so difficult that the local Trades Council made the strongest representation to the Managers on behalf of a group of anonymous nurses who had complained of being:

> underfed, ill-housed and working under conditions that would not be tolerated in any factory in the district.

They worked 75 hours per week instead of 48 and were paid no overtime. The response from the Managers was predictable enough — yes, the hours worked are long but shortage of nursing staff is widespread and they are trying to recruit. Yes, they are ill-housed but pending the building of the long promised Nurses Home the best they can be offered is the conversion of three war-time huts into cubicled temporary accommodation. No, they are certainly not ill-fed — the food in Falkirk Infirmary is first-class and the nurses and domestics get the same quality as the patients! And there the matter rested for the time being. The conversion of the wartime huts in 1946 cost £7,444 and by all accounts was a success providing each nurse with a separate bedroom as well as access to 'a lounge, writing room, baths, electric irons, hair-driers, wireless etc.' The cost was enough to turn a small overall surplus into a deficit for the year so the Managers agreed to fund the conversion from the money already gathered for the future nurses' home. As well as problems housing the nursing staff the Infirmary experienced difficulty recruiting the numbers they now required. In the same year an appeal was made for part-time helpers with nursing experience and during the month of October only emergencies were admitted to the Children's Ward. Miss Annie Gray Buchanan of Parkhill organised a nursing pageant in the Town Hall to try to drum up recruits to the profession but what impact it had is not clear. The numbers of nurses at the Infirmary hovered around the 100 mark for a few years and turnover was also high. In 1946 for example around 70 left Falkirk and 64 arrived. There were added financial demands as well of course arising from advances in provision and equipment — in 1947 Ward 1 was opened to cater for gynaecological cases and in the same year £6,794 was expended on up-to-date X-ray and darkroom apparatus.

Despite these post war difficulties for the staff, one can detect from the records and from the memories of the staff themselves, something of that special feeling of comradeship in adversity often reported by soldiers on the front line. Without minimising the real difficulties, there is no doubt that this shared experience of all the Infirmary staff laid the foundation for a post-war period marked out in the minds of those involved as a genuinely golden era in the history of the Infirmary. Perhaps it was the common hardship, or the enforced togetherness of young active people under firm discipline and severe stress, or the inspiring leadership from Dr Andrew Hunter and Matron Anna Dick. Whatever the reason the staff of Falkirk and District Royal Infirmary emerged from the dark days of the war with confidence to face an uncertain world.

The uncertainty arose primarily from the imminent nationalisation of all hospital services which had been promised by the Labour Party before the election of 1945 and signalled in the famous Beveridge Report of two years earlier. It was in reality more the concern of the Managers than the staff, for the medical and caring work would continue whatever management changes might be imposed. It was of course no great surprise. As early as 1930 the Managers were declaring their implacable opposition to any departure from the voluntary principle:

> It would indeed be a bad day for our Hospitals should they ever be taken over by the State or thrown upon the rates . . . . serious injury would be done to the welfare of the sick for whom the hospitals are provided, and the training of the medical profession and the progress of medical research.

But ten years of struggling for the massive sums now required to sustain a major general hospital forced a change of heart. Before the war the Chairman of the Board of Management, Colonel Alan Stein had suggested Government assistance for all voluntary hospitals and by 1940, when emergency procedures were at their height, he had concluded:

> The close co-operation between voluntary hospitals, the Department of Health, the local authorities which was the outcome of the present emergency may prove to be an important step towards the ideal of a national hospital service.

From then on there were regular statements from the Scottish Office, and from the Managers themselves, which came closer and closer to the kind of unified system embodied in the National Health Service (Scotland) Act 1947 which came into effect on the 5th July the following year. One Falkirk manager summed up the feeling of all the rest:

> If this nation thinks it can do a better job by nationalisation than we have done by voluntary methods then the nation must go ahead and prove it. We should not be down-hearted about change; we have had a good run and we have done a good job.

The 59th Annual Meeting in March 1948 was the last, and the Managers reaffirmed their view that the public support which had built and sustained the Infirmary for nearly sixty years would still be required in the days ahead:

> It is vital that the spirit of voluntary work should be kept alive and that thereby the Falkirk and District Royal Infirmary which has always been 'our' hospital shall remain 'our' hospital in the future.

The Infirmary was now part of the Western Regional Hospital Board, one of five in the country, to be run by a Board of Management for the Falkirk and District Hospitals with responsibility also for the Infectious Diseases Hospitals in Lochgreen Road and Camelon, the Denny and Dunipace Hospitals and Blinkbonny (later Winsdor) Home.

It is perhaps appropriate at this juncture to mention three individuals whose contribution to the growth of the Infirmary was almost inestimable. Firstly, Dr John Young, already mentioned, who retired as Medical Superintendent in 1947 after almost fifty years association with the Infirmary from its Cottage Hospital days. As President of the Infirmary in the 1920s he had played a principal role in the planning of the new buildings and in the years since they opened. If Dr Andrew Hunter drew the plaudits in ward or in theatre, it was John Young's political skills which secured the vital support in committee rooms and Council Chambers. Dr Young was succeeded for a brief period by Dr D A Lowe followed in February 1948 by Dr John Park, a Lanarkshire man with wide experience at home and overseas.

Dr John Young, Mr James Allan and Mr Duncan Kennedy

Mr Duncan Kennedy, the Infirmary's Honorary Secretary for twenty five years, died in September 1947 and it fell to his son Matthew to present the final annual report a few months later. Duncan was one of Falkirk's best known and most respected lawyers who gave over a great part of his life to the Infirmary. He masterminded the publicity which sustained the great fund-raising campaign in the 1920s and continued to keep the Infirmary in the forefront of the public's mind.

Most remarkable of all perhaps was James Allan, Honorary Treasurer for thirty-eight years and still in harness at the end of the period. The onerous task of ensuring that the contributions from diverse sources added up to the required expenditure was his lifetimes work from the time in 1910 when annual income was £1,500 through to 1947 when it topped £70,000. This unenviable task he carried out with total dedication and he deserves to be remembered along with John Young and Duncan Kennedy as one of the fathers of Falkirk and District Royal Infirmary.

The departure from the scene of these and other leading figures with long service in the voluntary years marked the change to a new style of administrative and financial management, but for the most part the caring work carried on unchanged. As the post-war reconstruction got underway, demand for hospital services continued

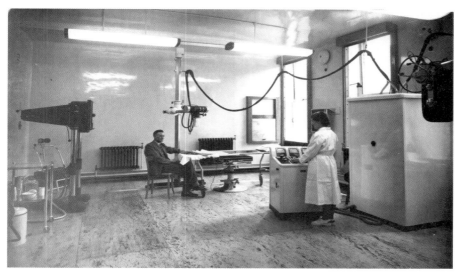

The new X-ray department

The opening of the new X ray unit with Provost Peter Symon, Sir Alexander Macgregor and Miss Gray-Buchanan among the guests

to grow and the huts became a permanent addition to the Infirmary's accommodation to be used at different times for patients, special medical services, administration or nurse training. The first major addition to the hospital's facilities came in 1951 with the opening of a new X-ray facility in a reconstructed ward. Over 150 invited guests gathered in the Recreation Hall to hear Sir Alexander Macgregor, Chairman of the Western Regional Hospital Board, declare the new unit open.   It was the first significant expenditure not met by public subscription and while the redoubtable Miss Annie Gray-Buchanan of Parkhill was on hand to present flowers to Lady Macgregor, the majority of those present were local councillors, MPs, administrators and hospital staff with very few of the old guard remaining. It was a new structure for a new age and welcomed by most, but with more than a hint of regret at the passing of a system which for all its inherent weaknesses had served the people of the district well for nearly sixty years.

CHAPTER SIX

A Golden Age

Although war-time emergencies stopped the construction of the new nurses home, the gathering of funds continued throughout the period and by 1945 the total stood at an impressive £75,000. As soon as post-war material shortages allowed, new plans were drawn up taking account of the advice of the Nursing Council. The result was a home of two buildings completed early in 1953 with accommodation for ten sisters, fifteen staff nurses and thirty six nurses. There were bed-sits for the juniors and what were called 'suites' for their more fortunate senior colleagues. Once again, as often in the past, the great and the good gathered to mark yet another official opening and, acknowledging that the money had been raised by the old voluntary method, the guests included many of the old Managers. Mrs James Allan, wife of the former Treasurer was the principal guest and there were many speeches, much nostalgia, several presentations and as ever 'a delightful tea'.

The following year brought the retiral of Matron Miss Anna Dick after twenty five years at the heart of the Infirmary. Throughout her time in Thornhill Road and Gartcows she was the embodiment of the spirit of determination and commitment which had overcome the most intractable of problems. She was an inspirational figure who shaped the lives of a generation of nurses and set the high standards of care and dedication on which her successors were able to build in the years which followed. In many ways her departure marked the final break with the past for her roots were in the old system and her links with the community were of necessity strong and influential. Life in the hospital changed as it continued to grow in size and complexity and more and more important decisions were taken outwith the district often by people who knew little of its make-up or traditions. But that was for the future.

The occasion of Miss Dick's retiral was a time for looking back on a

The new Nurses Home

Happy nurses and Sisters gather in front of their new home

special chapter in the Infirmary's history which is still fresh in the minds of many of the former nursing and medical staff today. It is not difficult to build up a picture of life for the doctors, nurses and patients as the Infirmary moved from the years of war into the 1950s and beyond. As we have already seen the nurses' hours were long and in addition they had to attend lectures in their own time. Although salaries were low they were required to pay for their own uniforms with the exception of the dresses which were pink for first year and blue for the other three. Staff nurses wore royal blue and ward sisters navy blue. The distinctive colours carried a significance beyond the obvious for the Infirmary was a fairly rigid hierarchy with the Matron and Senior Sisters held in considerable awe by the nurses who were left in no doubt as to what was expected of them, in their on or off-duty hours.

The early morning routine provides a good example. Breakfast for the day shift was at 7am precisely. Assistant Matron Miss 'Flossie' Wilson, the 'home sister' supervised proceedings in the staff diningroom where meals were served to the nurses sitting at tables

The Dining Room

The Sisters in 1959: Sr. Street, Sr. Kirk, Sr. Shanks, Sr. Porter,
Sr. Currie, Sr. Scotland, Sr. Bremner. Sr. Foreman, Sr. Petrie.

restricted to 'pink dresses', 'blue dresses', staff nurses or sisters. Woe
betide latecomers who arrived after the Matron or Senior Sister had
said grace and woe betide a nurse who left any part of the food or drink
unfinished. For much of the period it was egg one day, bacon the next
except Christmas Day and January 1st when the two came together in
a rare and welcome combination! Heaven help the nurse caught
pinching an egg from the tubs filled each year in 'Egg Month' by the
farmers of the carse, and stored in water-glass preservative for patients
use throughout the year!

While the nurses were on duty it was quite likely that Sister Wilson
would pay a visit to their quarters to ensure that they were tidy and
contained no unwelcome items or visitors. In the evening all nurses
had to be in by 10 pm and lights out was strictly at 11 pm. How many
sneaked in, or out, after these hours is not of course recorded, but over
the years the lure of the Cow Wynd chip shop must have drawn many
a hungry nurse from her cramped quarters, and no doubt the local
'talent' attracted more than a few stout-hearts into a highly risky
adventure in Doaks Dance Hall or the Saloon Picture House. Of

'intruders' to the Nurses' Home, either unwelcome or otherwise, lips remained sealed even after fifty years but Sister Elizabeth Shanks who was respected by all and feared by many tells one story of a visit to Gartcows House to inspect the nurses's rooms while they were at breakfast.

> I heard a rustling sound at the window and pulled back the cutains. There was a man clinging to the ivy with only his head and shoulders showing. He looked surprised to see me but he didn't say a word. He slithered away down the ivy and I heard his feet crunching the gravel as he made his escape.

She thought he was a 'peeping Tom' but much more likely just another Falkirk Romeo on his way in or out by arrangement with an unidentified Juliet somewhere inside the building!

For the most part however, nursing and domestic staff as well as the small number of resident doctors had to find their recreational activities within the Infirmary area. There are fond memories of the monthly dances in the Recreation Hall where the nurses in uniform, drank orange juice and irn-bru and danced to the music of the band led by Walter McLaren the Infirmary's Head Porter. Matron and Sisters dressed in evening gowns presided and many local doctors and others associated with the Infirmary were regular attenders. To a generation used to instant TV and Video entertainment, all-night discos and alcohol with everything, these monthly hops may seem tame to say the least, but they were a source of enormous fun and genuine enjoyment to those living in well

Head Porter Walter McLaren who led the dance band

nigh closed conditions. As well as the regular dances there were
Christmas Pantomimes when budding writers, singers and musicians
among the staff entertained one another with sketches and parodies
on Infirmary life — a chance for revenge on sister perhaps, or at least an
opportunity to ease the natural tensions which were present in the
day-to-day life of the nursing staff.

In the passing we should note that Walter McLaren also played the
piano for the weekly church services held alternately in Wards 3 and
4. In the wards the work routines were well established and strictly
observed and in addition to direct patient care there was much linen
checking, bandage preparation, needle sterilisation and bed-making
to fill the hours. One nurse remembers the range of nursing techniques
on offer:

> Patients with rheumatism were nursed in a blanket bed with a very
> narrow draw sheet in order to avoid chilling. Those with chest
> conditions like bronchitis and pneumonia were nursed in an upright
> position whereas cerebral conditions were kept completely flat with
> their heads placed between two sandbags to avoid undue movement.

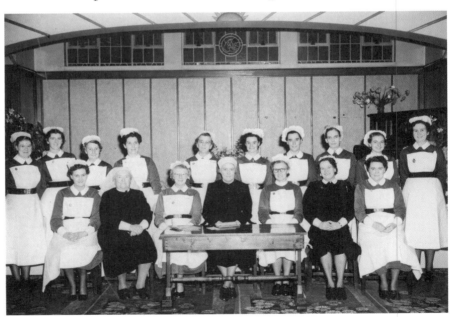

Miss Dick with her senior nursing staff in 1954

An early picture of Falkirk nurses in class

Nurses hours were long and time-off severely limited and, for those in training, unpaid after-duty sessions with nurse tutor 'Granny' Coutts, were a compulsory part of the day's work. From the 1940s on the Managers reported that nurse training was carried out 'on approved lines' and gave the number of nurses — usually between fifteen and twenty — passing the national examinations. Once they had completed their training the girls — and they were nearly all girls then — entered upon their hospital careers and, wherever they went, Falkirk Royal or elsewhere, they entered a highly regulated world. Craig Mair, in his new history of Stirling Royal Infirmary, quotes the historian Peter Ardern's description of that world in the 1950s:

> . . . . nursing was still traditional in terms of training and discipline. You still had Florence Nightingale values then and matron and sister had real authority. Matron then was as powerful as senior doctors. She had a bearing and an authority. Nurses living in nurse houses had to obey matron in their private life as well, taking instructions on how late they could stay out, how smartly dressed they were and the suitability of any young man they wished to marry – although getting married meant leaving the job.

Miss Anna Dick and Dr Andrew Hunter

Although Miss Dick seems to have earned the respect and affection of many she was certainly one of the old school. The resident doctors' rounds and the weekly visits by specialists were planned and well prepared for, but the sudden arrival of Matron unannounced must have provoked many a fluttering heart and flurry of activity. At times like these many were grateful that Miss Dick's Scottie dog Roddy which accompanied her on her rounds sat outside the ward door giving due warning of her presence to the sharp eyed nurses in the vicinity! No doubt when Roddy was not doing his tour of inspection he paid some attention to the Infirmary's other famous pet, a white cat owned by Miss Margaret Ainslie who ran the Infirmary kitchens. The superstitious nurses however, disliked 'Snowball' and tried at all times to keep the bad omen from the doors of their wards! Jessie McGregor who worked in the pharmacy at the time remembers that Roddy was subjected to a monthly enema administered by the Matron presumably to ensure that he did not disgrace himself during the rounds! Jessie also recalls how Miss Dick, while visiting Ward 2 would 'spy' on the Ward 3 nurses emptying the bedpans in the sluice room (known of course as the 'sloosh') in case they should be tempted to grab a fly smoke, which many were wont to do in those days.

Many other images from these years spring readily to mind — like orthopaedic TB patients sleeping outside in verandah beds in the coldest of winters, snug below their tarpaulin with tin hot water bottles, unharmed by the thin layer of snow or frost which covered them in the morning! Or of nurses queuing up to seek Matron's personal approval of a late pass or to pay over a precious sixpence to replace a broken thermometer. Or of Miss Dick meeting each patient as they were discharged to wish them well.

It would be easy to compile a whole book of anecdotes which illuminate the lives of staff and patients but these few glimpses must suffice for our present purposes. However, one aspect deserves further attention. In almost all the stories it is the personalities of certain individuals which shine through; and Andrew Tomney who joined the medical staff in 1942 as a resident and later spent twenty years as Consultant Surgeon, set down his memories of some of the doctors who had a special influence on him personally. His sharp eye and witty observation present us with a vivid picture of his colleagues and friends.

Andrew Tomney

Dr Hunter was undoubtedly the most respected doctor I have ever known. He lived nearby and despite a busy practice and being continuously on-call always appeared fresh, well rested, polite and unhurried. Affectionately referred to as 'Pop' he was beloved and respected by nursing staff, patients and doctors alike. On Monday evenings he always paid a ward round just to check that everything was in order for the next day when Mr Tennent would pay his round, see out-patients and do a theatre list. The rapport between these two men was quite remarkable and their contribution to the Surgical Department immeasurable. Dr Hunter had an amazing collection of anecdotes many of which still raise a laugh. He did his practice rounds on a motor cycle and wore leathers which he put on and took off in an extraordinary leisurely manner no matter the circumstances. In Dr Hunter the local doctors had a wise and good counsellor whom they much appreciated.

Miss Dick on her retirement with faithful Roddy by her side

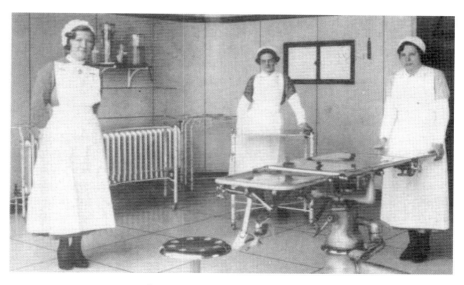

The Operating Theatre Staff

Sister Shanks also remembers Dr Hunter as often appearing quite late in the evening after the wards were settled down for the night. For him all the lights went back on but one suspects that a lesser mortal would have been given the proverbial flea in the ear. Among the surgeons one stood out for the young Tomney:

> Robert Tennent of the Victoria Infirmary, Glasgow, was visiting Consultant in my time and was the most dexterous surgeon I have ever had the pleasure of knowing. He was almost hyperactive and at times slightly impatient. Many found him to be rather formidable. Known to all as 'Lord Bob' he was generous in the extreme, paid ward rounds with remarkable swiftness absorbing everything and performed prodigiously in the Operating Theatre. His manipulative dexterity was remarkable and it was surgery's great loss that he died, burnt out with overwork at a comparatively early age. I remember him with respect and affection. When he visited Falkirk on Tuesdays he saw outpatients, then there was a luncheon when he and Dr Hunter revelled in witty conversation and verbal sparring. Afterwards he did a theatre list which often extended till late in the evening not uncommonly till 9.00 pm. Robert Tennent was the most remarkable craftsman I have ever known. He was my ideal.

Some remember 'Lord Bob' arriving from Glasgow by car and expecting the young resident doctor in surgery to be at the main door to greet him. Others recall his oft reported reply to the question of his family name: 'I'm not the beery Tennent, nor the soapy Tennent — I'm the bloody Tennent!' Then there was anaesthetist Dr Alex. Leitch:

> Known by all as the 'Plug' because he gave lectures on hygiene to nurses, Dr Leitch was also in General Practice. He was of a most distinctive appearance in that his eyebrows went up at their lateral ends. But he was a delightful character who loved his family, piano playing and opera. He was also keen on the work of William Shakespeare which he recited in theatre.

And pathologist Dr W. J. Logie known locally as the 'midnight doctor':

> He was in General Practice in Graham's Road and was extremely learned in the Classics, French and German. Theoretically he did pathology and the post mortems were done in a room off the basement corridor in the early hours of the morning. As he liked to have the company of a House Officer there was a captive audience for a lecture on the classics. He also had a reputation of never starting home visits until late at night, so much so that it is reported that an elderly lady living in Carron asked him to visit earlier as she was gaining a bad reputation with the neighbours on account of his late visits. He was a likeable character but I cannot ever remember receiving a report on any of the post mortems which he did.

Many of the nurses remember Dr Logie as a tall figure with silver hair and gold-rimmed spectacles who wore a long black smock while working late into the night. This appearance coupled with the nature of his trade was enough to severely shock many a young nurse meeting him by surprise in the basement corridor at two or three in the morning.

In Obstetrics and Gynaecology Falkirk Infirmary was served by Sir Hector McLennan assisted by brother ansd sister, Doctors Jean and John Horne both general practitioners in Denny. Andrew Tomney has special memories of them both:

> Jean was the essence of ladylike gentility but John was the more impressive and dynamic. I am told that his driving licence was not

of virgin purity as he had convictions for speeding. Minor accidents and bumps in the car were not infrequent. These were not unexpected as in the 1914-18 war he had been a pilot of distinction and contemporary of many of the famous flyers in the Royal Flying Corps. He was an excellent host and on many evenings his hospitality was greatly enjoyed. I admired him personally as a man, especially as I was one of the few who knew him to have performed a caesarian section on a patient with obstructed labour a few hours after his dear wife had died at home.

Finally there was the new Medical Superintendent, John Park whose arrival in 1948 coincided with Mr Tomney's return:

> He was a rather gruff individual and a great pigeon fancier. It was following one of his coronary episodes that the main corridor was covered with linoleum. Dr Park had found the noise of trolleys passing over the paving stones in the corridor rather noisy while he was incarcerated in Ward 5.

Dr Park's passion for his pigeons (or more correctly his 'doos') was well known to the staff and many remember how he would rush out of his office and head for home at anytime of the day if he heard that the 'doos' needed his attention. Meanwhile his faithful secretary Miss Simpson would deny all knowledge of his whereabouts until he returned with the birds safely back on their loft!

Of course Andrew Tomney was something of a character himself with a wicked sense of humour and a self-deprecating quality. Surgery he once said was closer to plumbing than medicine: 'I cut one pipe here and stitch another one up there. It's that simple!' He was a cigar smoker in the days before such practices were outlawed within hospitals and set off more that a few fire alarms. A well known FDRI legend persists that he even removed a patient's appendix while puffing on his favourite Havanna but few believe that he went quite that far! His wife Margaret who was a nurse in Falkirk Royal remembers how she would sneak out of the nurses' hut to meet him and, like more than a few young couples, found shelter in the old tennis pavilion in the grounds. Later he would lift her up and pop her back through the window. Such clandestine meetings were, of course, frowned upon especially ones involving two members of the staff!

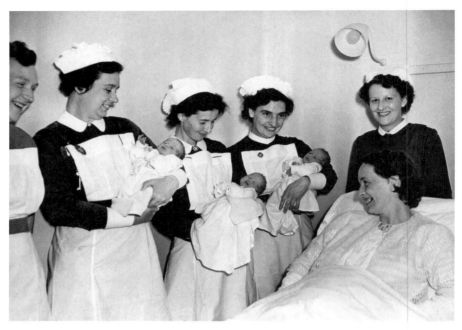

Falkirk Royal's First Triplets in 1956

Another eye witness to the life of FDRI was Jessie McGregor, already mentioned, whose work in the Pharmacy meant that she had contact with all the departments and most of the doctors and nursing staff over a period of thirty years or more.   She remembers the activities of the young doctors in their off duty hours which quite often featured the famous bust of Mrs Gibson which sat in the central stairwell.   No party inside the Infirmary or out in a pub seemed to be complete if the venerable old lady was not sitting in the centre of the table to 'bless' the proceedings.   It took two men to carry her so it was no easy undertaking but her presence was required so ways were found to allow her to attend.   Not infrequently on return she was deposited in some random spot leaving the furious porters to conduct a hospital wide search before carrying her back to the plinth.   One imagines that the frolics of the doctors were roundly cursed by those who had to do the heavy lifting.   Jessie recalls one case involving Doctors Bryce and Sinclair.   Miss Dick, the Matron, had found Mrs Gibson sitting on the lavatory pan in her private WC and fled along the corridor to the Medical Superintendent shouting 'Dr Park, Dr Park those bad boys

Mrs Gibson in her place on the stairwell

have been interfering with Mrs Gibson again!' Interestingly when the bust was removed for safe keeping to her family home in 2011 traces of lipstick and powder were found, evidence of her party-going days at FDRI!

Jessie also remembers men like T. Kay Maclachlan visiting physician in charge of Ward 2, female medical. He was ex-military and a formidable man by all accounts. The Ward Sister warned patients not to move when he was doing his rounds and on one occasion he looked at an over weight patient and snapped 'Tell me woman, is eating the only thing you do?' Bedside manner indeed. Then there was Mr Ronald Henderson a kind and caring man who had no airs or graces and was greatly mourned when he died suddenly while on a seminar trip to Scandinavia. Dr John Colvin is another fondly remembered as is 'Bert' Main senior surgeon who always wore his white coat collar up. More of him later in this story. And there were many more people doing a whole variety of jobs all of which contributed to the successful running of the hospital. Jessie remembers that there was a team of resident tradesmen whose task was to maintain the fabric of the building. Six painters, a bricklayer, a joiner, a plasterer and a plumber under the management of Clerk of Works George Allan looked after the Camelon and Denny Hospitals as well as Falkirk Royal.

Sometimes the memories were strong enough to inspire poetry: Marion Grant who worked in the out-patients department wrote the following lines which are part of a longer poem read out at the Centenary Dinner in 1990:

> I can remember just after the war,
> Our butter and sugar we kept in a jar,
> We heated the bed pans, the syringes we boiled,
> Disposables we knew not – oh how you are spoiled.
>
> Remember the classroom right under the ground,
> With dear Sister Coutts enormously round,
> Next, Callendar Park with Miss Steel known as Grace,
> Then back to the Royal – it is the best place!
>
> We all can remember Doc Bell and TK,
> Mr Main, Mr Henderson, the Hornes and 'Oh Lay',
> Remember our Sarah and Miss Dick with her dog,
> And J B when walking broke into a jog.

The difficult task of succeeding Miss Dick fell to Miss Sarah Chalmers from Glasgow's Southern General Hospital who took up her new post in 1954 and remained as Matron for twelve years. It proved to be a relatively quiet period in the Infirmary's history — the calm after the storms of war and nationalisation and before the turmoil of social and economic change which gripped the 1960s and beyond. There were few major changes until the very last year of Miss Chalmers service as the Infirmary staff and local Board of

Miss Sarah Chalmers

The new Physiotherapy Unit

Management came to terms with an administrative system radically different from what had gone before. Requests for new services or additional accommodation now took their place in a national queue and multi-million pound expenditure decisions were taken long miles from Falkirk and district. Miss Chalmers and her staff – there were by now over 170 nurses – were asked to serve a rapidly increasing population with limited additional resources and little prospect of a speedy improvement. In January 1957, on the 25th anniversary of the opening of the new Infirmary, over one hundred guests watched the Chairman of the Managers, ex-Provost Peter Symon, cut a special cake 'amid enthusiasm' and heard him declare his confidence in the Infirmary in the days ahead, despite the growth in demand which had seen in-patient numbers rise by half to over 6,000 in the decade after the war.

In 1959 Camelon Hospital was closed and the Geriatric Unit there moved to the Infirmary where two of the wartime huts were upgraded for this purpose. Space was also found for the fully equipped

Physiotherapy Unit to apply modern principles to the care of the elderly. The following year the Board of Management unveiled plans to tackle the Infirmary's biggest problem. A new showpiece out-patients department would be constructed to replace the inadequate existing facilities which could not cope with the doubling of out-patient numbers to over 20,000 per annum over the previous ten years. A sub-committee was formed to progress the plan and the reported that work would start in early 1962. In the event ten years, four general elections and several economic crises passed before work began but in the meantime there was one major development which put the name of Falkirk and District Royal Infirmary firmly on the map as far as modern hospital treatment was concerned. It was of course the now famous 'Falkirk Ward'.

CHAPTER SEVEN

Welcome Additions

In the late 1950 s the Scottish Home and Health Department began to re-examine the principles of ward design which had held sway for almost a century. The open 'Nightingale Wards' with rows of beds on either long wall had, or so it was said, serious 'functional weaknesses' and represented an approach to patient care which was out-dated and wasteful of staff and patient energy. The Department brought together what was called a 'multi-professional group' consisting of doctor, nurse, architect, engineer and work-study officer with instructions to design a modern ward. The result was the so-called 'race-track system' which the Department decided should be tried out in Falkirk and District Royal Infirmary by way of a half million pound experiment.

The new surgical unit

Thus was born the 'Falkirk Ward', a revolution in hospital patient care which brought more attention to Falkirk's Infirmary in the next five years than in the previous seventy five. Falkirk was chosen because the far-sighted managers of 1932 had provided sufficient land for expansion and because a request for additional surgical facilities had already been made to the Western Regional Hospital Board. No doubt the location of the Infirmary helped since it was within visiting, or perhaps striking distance, of Edinburgh where the Home and Health Department's experimentalists could watch developments. Whatever the reason the *Falkirk Herald* took the decision to be a vote of confidence in the Hospital:

> What is more important is that the local Infirmary has been selected for this development which puts Scotland in the forefront of modern planning because it has been recognised that Falkirk is the ideal place to carry out an extensive and intensive study of nursing work and patient requirements.

The new block consisted of a suite of operating theatres on the ground floor of the most modern design with two sixty bed units on the first and second floors. These were designed in single or four bed spaces separated from each other and built round a central area where

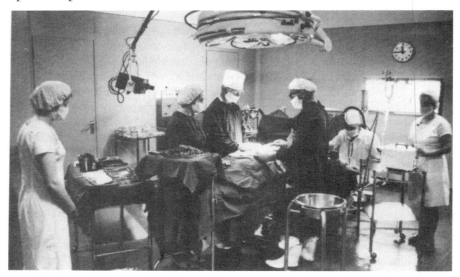

Robert Main and Andrew Tomney in the new surgical suite

The Princess of Nepal with Miss Cadger visit the Falkirk Ward

common facilities like the open nurses station, bathroom, stores, kitchen and preparation room were located. Each 'ward' had its own toilet and basin and there were day spaces where patients could spend time together talking or watching television. On 4th November 1966, the new block was opened by Mr Bruce Millan, then Under Secretary of State at the Scottish Office who declared that:

> In Scotland this is the biggest development project ever built in the health field as a practical expression of fundamental planning research studies.

Almost immediately the new wards became the magnet which drew visitors in their hundreds to the Infirmary from all over Scotland and beyond, and it was no six day wonder. In July, 1967 the *Scottish Daily Express* ran a main 'Photo News Extra' feature on 'One of the most modern operating theatres in Britain at Falkirk Royal Infirmary — Scotland's £400,000 theatre'. Nine months later the *Glasgow Herald*'s reporter was in town compiling a major article on the ward system

The nurses annual Christmas Carol visits to the wards
accompanied by a piano mounted on a trolley and under the
watchful gaze of the Matron and Sisters in the background.

which also featured the new nurses' uniforms which were:

> Speedwell Blue Dresses with their short sleeves and shirt style
> fastenings — easy to put on, comfortable to wear but shapeless
> and apt to make a plump girl look plumper.

They were doomed to failure and were replaced by the more
traditional white within a few years!

A few months after the new surgical unit opened Lena Sutherland
arrived in Falkirk Royal at the start of nearly 30 years service as a Staff
Nurse, Ward Sister and finally as a Health Service manager. She
found that some of the nurses were less than enthusiastic about the
new arrangements because 'they couldn't see the patients all the time
and patients missed seeing the nurses always in more or less constant
view'. But despite the new style of ward, the old tradition of consultant
ward rounds continued with the poor patient lying quietly in bed while
a team of doctors discussed their case. Central to this important
activity was, of course, the head of surgery Mr Robert Main:

> Every Wednesday morning he conducted a round of the patients
> who were in the care of the general surgeons. He expected every

Surgical Consultant to attend these rounds along with the Registrar, Senior house officer, Junior house officer and Ward Sister. The consultants discussed their patients with each other and the junior medical staff were expected to contribute in these discussions The ward sister reported on how the patient was responding to the care. These rounds were good in allowing discussion on the different aspects of the care and instructions usually given on any changes.   Mr Main was an excellent Surgeon and expected a high standard of everyone in his team and that included how they presented themselves on the ward.   I well remember a charming young female house officer, straight from university eagerly attending the ward round wearing a smart pair of trousers and top under her white coat. Mr Main, in front of the whole retinue quietly told her to leave the ward round and return when she was appropriately dressed. Women wearing trousers! That constituted a drop in standards. I did feel sorry for the young doctor who looked mortified; she had the makings of a good doctor and I am sure has gone on to greater things. By the time I retired [1996] the ward rounds were less structured and consultants could arrive on any day at any time and tended to work individually. Pressure of work influenced this change but we did loose something of the team effort and sharing of knowledge that we had with the more formal ward rounds.

In the meantime the Matron Miss Chalmers had reached her retirement and had remained an extra year to see the new wards opened. Now with the project safely launched she finished her time in Falkirk and retired to her native town of Leven. Her successor was Miss Agnes Cadger from Aberdeenshire who had come to Falkirk as assistant to Miss Chalmers in 1963 from a similar post in the Southern General Hospital. The task facing her was particularly difficult for not only was Falkirk Infirmary the focus of much attention from the outside world but it was now, with 420 beds, 350 nurses and nearly 100 domestic staff, a bigger and infinitely more complex organisation that at any time in its long history. The expectations of staff and patients in the late 1960s were far removed from the benign acceptance of inadequacies of an earlier age and the staff were no longer to be managed by methods which had kept generations of their predecessors up to the mark. To this task the new Matron brought precisely the right

Miss Chalmers' Retiral Presentation

combination of qualities with a firm grounding in the old school virtues of dedication and discipline enhanced by a patient and understanding nature.

A few months after Miss Cadger took over at least one group of her staff had cause to celebrate when sixteen nurses and three sisters moved into five newly built villas in Gartcows Drive. Their new accommodation was of very high quality but it did not come cheap as the local paper reported:

> Full-board student nurses will pay £143 per year out of a salary of £365 upwards. Ward sisters will pay £265 out of their salary which is between £690 and £850.

In September 1968 a new baby care unit was opened to provide special facilities for babies born prematurely or with conditions requiring immediate treatment. All babies born in the maternity ward were sent to one of three nurseries in the unit for their first thorough examination. In the late 1960s over 2,300 babies were born each year

Dr Bell and Miss Cadger with prize-winning nurses in 1967

in Falkirk Royal and in 1971 a prefabricated neo-natal unit was built onto the maternity wing thus releasing space in the existing unit for five labour rooms. Despite this addition, the adequacy of the whole maternity provision was called into question within a few years. High level meetings involving the Home and Health Department, the Infirmary's Board of Management and the Regional Hospital Board confirmed that the unit built in 1932 was indeed inadequate and that overcrowding and long waiting lists for gynaecological treatment were unacceptable. When a Government Minister suggested that mothers-to-be might have to travel to the new unit at Stirling Royal Infirmary, it provoked a furious reaction in the district, and outraged local MPs asked questions in the House of Commons. By the middle of 1973 the *Evening News* was announcing 'Falkirk Wins Maternity Beds Battle!' with one other contender, Cumbernauld, the loser.

In the moment of triumph campaign leader Harry Ewing MP sounded a suitable note of caution:

I hope the unit will be built as soon as possible. It is of course impossible to indicate with any certainly at this stage of planning when the new unit will be operational.

In the event another ten years came and went before the work was underway. In the meantime the long awaited out-patient department promised back in 1961 was completed in February, 1973. Described as a 'pioneer project' and a 'revolutionary planning idea' the out-patients section was intended to streamline the processing of the 140,000 out-patient visits each year so that they received better treatment, quicker attention and greater privacy in more spacious and pleasantly furnished accommodation. The two storey building with out-patients on the upper level and a new look accident and emergency department below cost nearly £800,000 and employed an additional eighty staff. Special features included a sixteen bed short-stay unit for overnight stays, six X-ray rooms, eighteen consulting rooms as well as two dental suites and two rooms for ophthalmology.

The Accident and Emergency Department contained a Resuscitation Room, eight examination/treatment rooms and access to a new operating suite designed as a full scale theatre with all the facilities available in the main hospital. Despite this major step forward and the promised replacement of the Maternity Unit, the Infirmary

Miss Cadger and Mr Main with a new TV for the Chidren's Ward

The new Out Patients and Accident and Emergency Building

continued to face accommodation difficulties in the mid 1970s. The waiting lists continued to grow to over 1,700 and Senior Consultant, John Colvin, claimed that another 200 beds would be required to solve the problem:

> Recently we were forced to crowd the medical wards with extra beds in the middle of the floor. And eventually we may have to put patients in corridors.

Greater life expectancy also led to increased demand for geriatric beds and once again the Falkirk area was short of provision. Lack of money was blamed and again local MPs quizzed the Secretary of State on future plans but this time no extravagant promises were made and the Infirmary staff had to make the best of space made available in the old out-patients and accident departments.

By then there had been two significant management changes. The planned creation of Central Regional Council brought in its wake a much heralded and long debated health service restructuring. The Stirlingshire Hospital Board which had only been in existence for a few years was replaced in April, 1974 by the Forth Valley Health Board. The Board took over responsiblity for both Falkirk and Stirling Infirmaries plus all other health care facilites in Stirlingshire and

Clackmananshire. Its headquarters, which like those of its predecessor body were in Stirling, relocated to the former Royal Infirmary building in Spittal Street. One of the Board's earliest announcements was the addition of thirty surgical orthopaedic beds at a cost of £100,000 in part of the newly freed hutted accommodation at the Infirmary and this did go someway to easing the problems of overcrowding, but long waiting lists remained.

The other change which came about at this period was the introduction of the Salmon Scheme for senior nursing posts, which among other things, brought an end to many old familiar titles. It was to be good-bye Matron after eighty years in Falkirk and welcome Principal or Senior Nursing Officer! Days of sex equality and an increasing number of male nurses in the service brought doubts about titles like 'Matron' and 'Sister' and the neutral names were the result. The changes were not welcomed by many and it was clear that staff, patients and the general public preferred the friendly and familiar, but while few endorsed the new approach, it was imposed. Of all the changes faced by the staff at this time one stands out as an example of how something which seems relatively trivial can generate a great deal of irritation and even resentment. This was, of course, the question of the nurse's uniform. Traditionally the white aprons and starched collars, and especially the hats, confirmed the status of the wearer. Different colours of trim on the hat meant something significant to the staff and indeed to the patients while the Sisters and the Matron were instantly recognisable. The people making the decisions decided that all of this was old fashioned and so off with the hats and on with a clean overall dress each day. It was another blow at long cherished symbols and, like Salmon, helped drive down morale at a time when maximum co-operative effort was required.

But it was not these cosmetic change however controversial which were the most significant. More importantly, the new scheme reflected a fundamental shift in the way large and complex institutions like infirmaries were now organised and managed. Professional managers now controlled administration while catering and domestic services had their own specialists in charge. It was a new world far removed from the era when the matron reigned supreme, and inevitable and necessary as these developments no doubt were they were never particularly welcome and their growth in the 1970s and '80s was a watershed in the history of the Infirmary.

Nowhere was this change better illustrated than in the field of administration. Back in the pre-Health Service days secretarial and financial matters were dealt with from the law offices of Duncan Kennedy and James Allan and a similar arrangement continued into the 1950s. In the Kennedy family law offices in Princes Street and later in Wellside Place, a small group of staff maintained financial and staff records for the rapidly growing Infirmary with Matthew Kennedy acting as Secretary to the Board of Management. In 1962 John Wallace was appointed Group Secretary and Treasurer to the Falkirk and District Hospitals Board with a new office in the former day room at the end of one of the wooden huts erected during the war. A few months later, the administration staff moved from Wellside Place to the Infirmary. Jessie McGregor, Nessie McGaw, Nancy Rice, Jean Milne, Jean Suttie, Helen McDonald, Nicol Ferguson and others gave many years of valuable service to the Infirmary and witnessed a whole series of changes as management structures came and went. In 1962 Robert Gibson became the first Hospital Secretary and he was followed by Douglas Caldwell, Alistair Barton and Brian Baillie. Each successive structure brought further change from a district office, to a unit of the Forth Valley Health Board, right down to the Unit Management Team of 1983. By the end of that decade the Unit General Manager Bill Blackie had a staff of 150 responsible for the full range of administrative and secretarial services required to manage a modern hospital with nearly 1,400 medical, nursing and support staff.

The 1970s brought the retirement of a number of well known personalities and while it would be impossible to name them all in this short survey there were a number whose departure attracted the attention of the local press. They came from all parts of the hospital service and so, for us here, they can perhaps represent all their colleagues whose loyal service helped to build and sustain Falkirk and District Royal Infirmary in the decades after the war.

In 1972, William Mitchell, 'House Steward' for twenty-four years retired and shortly afterwards sister Elizabeth Bremner ended twenty-six years as Sister in charge of the Out Patients Department. Miss Bremner trained in Falkirk in the 1930s returning in 1946 to the

Mr Main presents a retirement 'scroll' to Sister Bremner

Infirmary. Dubbed 'Miss Falkirk Royal' by Dr Bell, Miss Bremner was honoured by all her colleagues at a special presentation when her long service was recalled and presentations made by the Matron, the Senior Surgeon, Senior Physician and representatives of the nursing and clerical staff and the local Board. Three months later Dr William Bell was himself on the receiving end of the honours when his own long career spanning forty one years came to an end. Dr Bell joined the staff shortly after the new Infirmary opened, served throughout the war and ended his outstanding service as Senior Consultant Physician. For more than two decades he was at the hub of the Infirmary leading the medical team and representing the institution very effectively to the world outside. Well known and highly respected his departure was a great loss to Falkirk.

Another very well known member of staff reached retirement in 1974 after over thirty years service. Miss Margaret Weatherhead, the Almoner, gave invaluable assistance to patients whose illnesses brought with them social or financial problems. Now described as a Medical Social Worker – though she would not thank you for using the term –

Miss Weatherhead had a seemingly insatiable appetite for helping others – apart from her work she helped found the Samaritan Society to give emergency help to discharged patients, assisted in the foundation of the Old Peoples' Welfare Committee, served as an independent Councillor on Falkirk District Council for four years and was an active member of the Soroptimist Club of Falkirk. In the same month Hospital Secretary Robert Gibson left after twelve years and one year later it was the turn of Superintendent Radiographer, Margaret Dalziel after more than thirty years in the hospital service.

In 1976 the twenty-seven year service of the Infirmary's Senior Consultant Surgeon Robert G. Main was ended by his own ill health and early retirement. Seven years earlier Mr. Main was honoured by the award of the OBE in the New Year's Honours List for services to medicine and in recognition of his work in the planning and evaluation of the 'Falkirk Ward'. During his long career Mr Main had also made an extensive contribution to the scientific aspects of surgery and one such was dealt with in a paper entitled 'The Surgical Treatment of Molten Metal Burns from the Falkirk Foundries', obviously still of great concern many decades after Patrick Tully's historic injury back in 1889. Another well known doctor honoured for his work in both Falkirk and Stirling Infirmaries was Consultant Paediatrician Robert

Dr William Bell with the year's top nurses

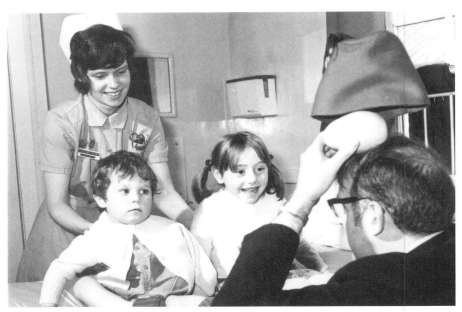

A mixed reception for the entertainer in the children's ward

Lulu pays a visit to the children accompanied by Alistair Barton

Spiers whose pioneering work linking thalidomide with the disastrous consequences of its use, brought the OBE in 1979.

The late 1970s brought difficult days for the whole country and it was not long before the discontent and anti-government sentiments had a direct effect on the life of Falkirk Royal. The so called 'winter of discontent' which saw a prolonged dispute between the public sector trade unions and the Labour Government was marked by a series of strikes including thousands of support workers in hospitals. Porters catering and domestic staff were involved and, as it happened, their action co-incided with a prolonged spell of severe winter weather which stopped many nurses and doctors getting to work on time or at all. Lena Sutherland was by this time one of the managers of the Infirmary and she remembers New Years Eve and the unfolding crisis:

There were two managers designated to be on site during this period and I was one of them. I should have started my shift at 1pm on Hogmanay. Normally the drive into work took 20 minutes. The car had to be abandoned and between buses, trains and walking I finally arrived at 2pm, much to the relief of my colleague who should have been off duty at 1pm. We quickly realised that everyone was having the same travelling difficulties and we started planning combined cars etc to get staff in and arranging overnight stay for staff who offered to stay on if needed. My colleague and I were on duty, practising crisis management from Saturday lunch time until the end of the New Year holiday break on the following Tuesday. Apart from the transport difficulties of getting staff in and then home to their young families we were short of linen, had only a skeleton domestic staff, and were, of course, short of staff at ward level. But the Dunkirk spirit prevailed. Managers who could, came in to help as did staff who lived within walking distance. The police were ever helpful with their 4 wheel drives in taking staff home and bringing them in.

We helped in the wards with the care of the patients while responding to calls from staff trying to get in and arranging pick-ups. I well remember Miss Blackwood our Director of Nursing doing her domestics in cleaning ward sinks and toilets and Doctors helping to deliver clean linen. We ran out of mortuary space as the holiday weekend and grave diggers strike resulted in a backlog of bodies waiting to be buried. The funeral parlours were most helpful!! We started to have a thaw, the roads improved and staff were returning from the long weekend break. But the strike continued. Managers and Consultants had to help in keeping the service running albeit an emergency service by this time. All waiting list admissions were cancelled. Nurse managers and other service managers with consultants were on a rota to do portering, domestic, and catering duties. The doctors seemed to be thoroughly enjoying themselves dishing up patients' meals and delivering them on trolleys to the respective wards.

In his history of Stirling Infirmary Craig Mair says that the Stirling Royal Matron, Miss Margaret Plenderleith, who presumably could not reach Stirling, spent a long day in Falkirk Royal peeling potatoes! It was further proof that whatever the merits of the public workers' case — and there were many — the nursing staff and their managers

The Matron and Sister Lucy Balmer watch a young patient try out a new ward telephone, one of many gifts to the Infirmary.

were not prepared to see patients suffer and would pull out all the stops to ensure that they were given the best care possible, while respecting their colleagues' right to fight for fair treatment

But for the tens of thousands of patients for whom the Infirmary brought new life and hope, relief from pain and comfort in distress it was the day to day support of hundreds of dedicated staff which meant more than buildings opened, extensions promised for the future or retirement presentations. All through the '70s as delays brought overcrowding and deteriorating conditions the caring work of the Infirmary went on as domestic staff as well as consultants, staff nurses and junior doctors, porters and dozens of other professionals combined to create the community of Falkirk and District Royal Infirmary which remained 'our Infirmary' to the people of the district as it had done in both triumph and adversity for over ninety years.

CHAPTER EIGHT

A Much Changed World

The first significant event of the new decade was another farewell, for in 1981 Miss Agnes Cadger, Matron from 1966 to 1972 and thereafter Senior Nursing Officer, reached retirement. She had presided over the Infirmary during its busiest and most difficult period and commanded enormous respect not only from her colleagues but throughout the town and the district. From her earliest months in Falkirk, Miss Cadger was guided by a certainty that she was called to serve the people here and she held fast to this conviction throughout her years of service and continues to do so in an active and caring retirement. Gentle but firm, dedicated and compassionate, quietly spoken though forthright and determined, she had all the gifts and gave them freely to all who came her way.

The highlight of the activities marking Miss Cadger's retirement was one very memorable night when the Rev James Currie produced the famous 'Red Book' at a surprise party and announced to his startled victim 'Agnes Cadger, This is Your Life'. In front of sixty colleagues and friends her nursing career was reviewed including the sixty-five mercy flights on the Air Ambulance Service and her eighteen years service in Falkirk. 'It was', said Mr Currie, 'the moving story of a truly wonderful woman and a dedicated nurse'. For Miss Cadger her place of retirement was

Miss Agnes Cadger

no far retreat but a house overlooking the main entrance to the Infirmary where she still keeps a watchful and sometimes worried eye on the institution she served with such devotion.

The task of leading the nursing team now fell to Miss Jean Blackwood whose official title was Divisional Nursing Officer. Immediately she was plunged into the arrangements for an official opening and Ministerial visit. In January 1982, Mr Allan Stewart, Parliamentary Under Secretary of State for Scotland came to perform a double service. Firstly, he declared open a new Post Graduate Education Centre and there unveiled a plaque. The Centre had been created over the previous eight months from the area which had housed the Infirmary's

Miss Jean Blackwood

original operating theatres and had more recently been used for laboratories. Costing over £70,000, the new Centre now provided the medical and nursing staff with up to date lecture and seminar rooms for study and research purposes.

A further ceremony awaited Mr Stewart on the main staircase of the Infirmary where, under the stony gaze of Mrs J E Gibson he marked the fiftieth anniversary of the new Infirmary by unveiling a second plaque. Later he visited Maternity B ward where he presented the mothers of six babies born on the 18th January with an engraved christening cup. Then it was the turn of the senior citizens when in the Ward 3 sitting room the Minister presented the oldest female patient Margaret Smith, aged 95, with an engraved pewter goblet and the oldest male, Robert Hughes, aged 94, with an engraved pewter mug.

If the people of the district were taking a greater interest than usual in their Infirmary at this time it was not only the response to a fiftieth anniversary. Provost John Docherty's great Hospital Appeal launched in February 1981 was reaching its climax and a last gasp effort to achieve the £50,000 target was underway. The aim had been to raise enough

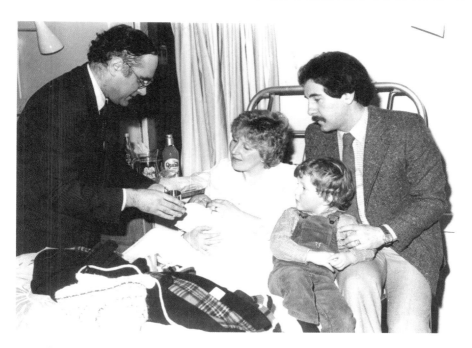

Allan Stewart MP presents a Christening Cup in January 1982

Mr Robert Hughes receives his commemorative pewter goblet

money to provide a special bus for geriatric patients, an orthopaedic operating table, a special microscope for eye surgery and specialised beds for geriatric patients, and the appeal had attracted widespread support. The *Falkirk Herald*'s headline 'Togetherness' reaffirmed the link between the people and the Infirmary which had sustained it for over 90 years. Throughout the year individuals and organisations arranged fund-raising activities with the highlight a Family Day in August in Callendar Park attended by 15,000 people which added £5,000 to the fund. Elaborate plans were made to bring the Duke of Kent to Falkirk on the fiftieth anniversary of the Infirmary's opening to present the £50,000 to the hospitals but in the end these hopes were dashed. In February 1982 when the appeal finally ended the Provost himself handed over the cheque which was, he said, tangible proof of the togetherness called for at the start of the campaign.

For one group of people in the district, fund raising for the hospital was nothing new; indeed the year the Provost's Appeal reached its target, the loyal and devoted Friends of the Falkirk and District Hospitals Association clocked up their Silver Jubilee. Founded in 1957 as a completely voluntary organisation, the Friends sole objective was to help the Royal Infirmary and the Burgh and Windsor Hospitals. This was done by providing much needed equipment over the years — ambulifts to aid the handling of very ill geriatric patients, infusion pumps, resuscitators and other special instruments for

James Clark

gynaecology, and a number of fully equipped emergency trolleys. There was a considerable amount of furniture, thousands of books for the library and a library service to all wards twice each week. There were toys and games for children, Christmas presents galore and coach trips for the elderly. All of this was provided by the fund-raising Friends and the donations they received from the public — over £100,000 by 1982 — and much of the credit for their enormous contribution must go to their long serving Chairman, Mr James Clark, who had worked tirelessly to keep the needs of the hospital in the public mind.

But the Friends were not alone. Many other organisations and countless individuals carried on the tradition established in the old voluntary days by devoting their time, energy and ingenuity to the task of fundraising or providing vital support services to the Infirmary. The Womens Royal Voluntary Service led the way with a whole range of activities including the much loved trolley service to the wards and the shop in the out-patients department. The WVRS members remain a welcome and familiar part of the Infirmary scene and the debt owed to them by the community is enormous.

But a glance through local newspapers of the period underlines the extent of the other support available to staff and patients. Inner Wheel, Women's Guilds, Rotary and Round Table, Scouts and Guides and a host of other groups, are regularly seen handing over vital pieces of equipment or funds to improve the quality of the Infirmary's environment. By the 1980s such sums exceeded £80,000 per annum in addition to the amount raised by Jim Clark and the Friends.

It was appropriate then that the special twenty-fifth anniversary gathering of the Friends was the first to hear the news for which they had waited for more than ten years. Local MP, Harry Ewing, announced that the long promised Maternity Unit, plus a new Geriatric facility, had been approved at last at an estimated cost of £6.4 million. Work was expected to start at the end of 1982 but again the project was delayed and conditions in the Infirmary continued to deteriorate. A desperate shortage in the General Medical wards led in April 1983 to the transfer of twenty-six beds from Ward 6, Gynaecology, leading to delays and protest in that area and the Health Board announced plans for a new thirty bed Acute Ward at the cost of £500,000. As well as increasing facilities at Falkirk Royal this new unit would release a number of beds at Lochgreen Hospital for long stay patients. In the meantime the staff had to cope as best they could, powerless to prevent the build up in waiting lists which were a feature of the mid 1980s. Dr Len Graham, the Health Board's Chief Medical Officer, put his finger on the main problem:

> We have simply been unable to keep pace. The influx, of geriatric patients has had a snowball effect throughout the whole place

By the end of 1983 there were over two thousand patients on the waiting list nearly half had been there for six months or more. Only the new accommodation would solve the problem and, in the Spring of 1984, further details of the plans were unveiled. The Maternity Unit would provide 56 beds, 15 special baby-care cots and 6 delivery rooms, and the Geriatric Unit 120 beds and a Day Hospital. The three storey block occupying a 3 acre site would now cost over £8 million and would be ready at the end of 1986. Forth Valley Health Board Chairman, Graham Horsman cut a cake in the shape of the new unit and the staff began to believe that the long promised units were on their way at last. Construction work began a few weeks later and continued for the next thirty months, during which time the staff and patients made the best of living and working next door to the building site.

As if to underline the fact that the caring work of the Infirmary went on whatever the situation came the response a few months later to one of the district's biggest disasters of the modern era. On 30th July 1984, the 5.30pm express train from Edinburgh to Glasgow was derailed by a bullock straying onto the line near Polmont. In the ensuing carnage 13 people died and 70 were injured, some seriously. It was Scotland's worst rail accident for nearly half a century and Falkirk Royal was the nearest hospital, and the receiving centre for the dead and injured. Lena Sutherland was the duty manager that night and she recalls that some time before an official call came from the police one of the porters had picked up from somewhere a rumour of the disatrous events a few miles away. Lena alerted Dr Bill Thomson who was the medical manager and soon afterwards the official emergency disasters plan was put into practice. Calls went out to off duty medical staff and a team was immediately assembled and equipped for transport to Polmont. When consultants arrived at the Infirmary they set about speedy rounds of the wards to see who could be discharged to free up emergency beds and soon the casualties began to arrive. By this time staff had come in numbers and by careful relocation of existing patients it was possible to create a specialist area where all those from Polmont were able to receive the intensive treatment they required. About 15 seriously injured patients were treated plus many more 'walking wounded' in A & E. The emergency planning had been put to the test in a real life or death situation and it had performed extremely well.

A year before these events Falkirk Royal had received yet another boost when the Forth Valley Health Board decided in early 1983 to site their new £1 million custom built College of Nursing and Midwifery on the Gartcows site rather than at Wellgreen in Stirling. Once again the wisdom of the founding fathers providing for future expansion had paid off for Falkirk. When finished the College would provide places for 600 nurses in training for all the Board's hospitals and thus continue the long involvement of Falkirk Royal with nurse training begun in the 1920s and continued with such distinction in the intervening years.

The new Maternity and Windsor Unit opened in April 1987

By April 1987 the new Maternity and Geriatric Unit was ready for occupation and in October of the same year it was officially declared open by the Scottish Health Minister, Michael Forsyth. With the Geriatric Unit now fully operational the old Windsor Hospital was no longer required and it closed its doors in 1988. The new facility at Falkirk Royal was named the Windsor Unit and continuity with the past was preserved. A few weeks later it was the turn of yet another Government Minister to do the honours when Lord Glenarthur visited Falkirk for the official opening of the new College of Nursing and Midwifery. The splendid new facilities which replaced those at the former Callendar Park College of Education include a lecture theatre,

Forth Valley College of Nursing and Midwifery

library and computer suite, as well as the usual range of seminar and classrooms, practical areas and a restaurant.

These two major projects were not the only new provision to come the way of the Infirmary in the late 1980s. Over £1 million was allocated to a new Sterilisation and Disinfection Unit, £500,000 for an extension to the Pharmacy and a similar sum for an Obstetrics and Gynaecology clinic. It was in total a £18 million commitment to Falkirk Royal providing facilities on a par with any provincial hospital in the land. It was, of course, an increasingly difficult task to maintain such standards for, in the words of Lewis Hynd, Chairman of the Health Board 'medical and hospital technology is changing at an astonishing speed and patients needs and expectations are also changing'. By the centenary year, 1989, annual expenditure topped £20 million and the Infirmary was employing 750 nursing staff and 350 staff in catering, domestic and portering duties.

Throughout 1989 special events marked the centenary year and staff at all levels in the organisation threw themselves energetically into the various commemorative activities which will be fresh in the minds of the participants and the people of the district. Dinners and dances, pageants, a Burns Supper, historical displays, scarves and teeshirts, commemorative mugs and a host of other events and special items marked the achievement of one hundred years of continuous service and, through it all, through all the celebrations, the day-to-day caring work of the Infirmary went on as it always had in the past.

The Centenary Cake

The contrast between Mrs Gibson's little cottage hospital of 1889 and the massive Falkirk and District Royal Infirmary of 1989 could not have been greater. Then a couple of nurses looked after a handful of patients in two small wards with no facilities to speak of and only the services of an odd visiting doctor. Now, [in 1989], tens of thousands of patients, hundreds of staff in all manner of specialisms with state-of-the-art equipment in modern and spacious accommodation. And of course the growth continued apace up to the present day.

Inevitably then the task facing the observer trying to describe and explain all of this change becomes more and more difficult as the years pass and the complexity of the organisation continues to increase. In the confines of a short account like this it is impossible to do justice to the huge range of activities, the number of specialisms, and the twists and turns of structure, governance and clinical practice which mark the growth and development of the last two decades. Whereas it was possible before to name names, describe most changes in layout etc. and to celebrate each new advance, now we must settle for an outline of the major concerns which preoccupied the staff and managers on the twenty year journey to the future in the shape of the magnificent new Forth Valley Royal Hospital. What follows then comes with apologies to those who may say 'He never mentioned so and so', or 'How could he forget to include the work of such and such and her team?' That will be the task of someone else in the future when the distance of time allows for proper reflection and for the proper sifting and analysis of the massive amount of information generated in our statistics driven age.

Mrs Iris Isbister , Chairman of Forth Valley Health Board, opens the new Maternity Out-patients department in 1989 accompanied by Central Regional Convener, Charles Snedden, Provost Dennis Goldie of Falkirk and local MP Dennis Canavan

As the staff and community joined in celebration of the first hundred years they had much to be optimisic about. The new facilities added during the previous decade had kept Falkirk Royal as well provided as any hospital outwith the great cities and, despite the economic woes of the country and the unsettling effect of continuous change in management structure the outlook remained bright. However there was one nagging problem which had never been far from the surface for many years, even decades. The clinicians in Forth Valley had long been convinced that the combined population of around 250,000 was only half of what was required to sustain one major acute hospital far less two. There was much talk of a 'critical mass' of people needed to ensure that specialists would have enough opportunity to practice their skills, with the implication that if they could not then they would leave for somewhere where such opportunities were available. Such discussions though well known in hospital circles were not however in wide circulation among the public and when they were the conclusion that was drawn caused a major furore. In January 1989 the *Falkirk Herald* ran a front page story with the startling headline 'Health Chiefs may Close Hospital'. The story which followed was based on a report from a group of doctors established by the Forth Valley Health Board and the Area Medical Committee to examine future challenges facing the Board. The long debated question of acute hospital provision was discussed and the group expressed the view that a single hospital for the Forth Valley at some time in the future was probably inevitable. It was really no more than that — a vision of the future, perhaps thirty or forty years ahead. But that didn't really matter. The headline was what people read and, on the basis of little or no evidence, 'They are going to shut down our hospital' became the cry picked up quickly by politicians both local and national. The explanations and denials which the Health Board issued were ignored or not believed and thereafter every pronouncement made at local and county level was carefully scrutinised. The assumption was made immediately that if there was to be one hospital it would be based around Stirling Royal and that Falkirk would be the loser

Part of the reason for the negative reaction lay in the history, and especially the recent history, of relations between Falkirk and Stirling. In Falkirk there was a long standing conviction, widely shared, that 'Stirling' who or whatever that meant, was hell bent on 'besting' Falkirk as often, and in as many ways as possible. Conspiracy theorists pointed to the location of the new University, and the Headquarters of Central Regional Council, Central Scotland Police, Forth Valley Enterprise and the Health Board itself. All were in Stirling while the population, and some claimed, the income generation, lay in the Falkirk area. Add to that the Thistle Centre pinching customers from the 'bairns' shops and you had a potent mix in which there seemed little room for rational debate on the true merits of the case. For those responsible for managing health care in the whole area this was just another difficulty which had to be overcome by patience and diplomacy and with a sensitivity to the genuine feelings of the people of both towns. It was a task which occupied much time over the succeeding years and began within days of the alarmist reports in the press.

Within a week of the *Herald*'s story campaign groups had been formed and declarations of support for Falkirk Royal poured in to the *Herald* from politicians, clergymen and the general public. The Provost promised to lead a sit-in at the Infirmary if necessary:

> If there is any threat to Falkirk Infirmary the fight will not just be from nurses, staff and patients. It will be the whole community fighting with every means at our disposal.

In February over 2000 people marched through the town in protest and at the rally which followed heard the late (and great) Harry Ewing MP make the astonishing promise:

> If all our arguments fall on deaf ears I'll put my political beliefs aside and we'll take over the hospital and run it ourselves.

Such rhetoric, however unrealistic the proposals it contained, was in tune with the mood of the crowds who cheered the speakers and pledged to fight to the last. In response, the Health Board denied they had any such plans and pointed out that in the previous year they had allocated £2 million to the hospitals of which Falkirk had received threequarters. Michael Forsyth, Minister of State at the Scottish Office, and Stirling MP, was quoted as saying that it would be 'bonkers' to close either of the hospitals and this helped ease the minds of some though most remained sceptical. In the Autumn a new report reached the public domain and this further inflamed the situation. The Health Economics Research Unit at Aberdeen University had been commissioned by FVHB to appraise the options for future provision and had concluded that one hospital for Forth Valley was by far the best outcome. The 'Save Falkirk Health Service' campaign held a packed and 'emotive' meeting in the Town Hall and a huge petition was launched which by the summer of 1990 had accumulated 53,000 signatures. But by the time it was delivered to the Scottish Office in Edinburgh, Forth Valley Health Board had announced that it had felt 'a very strong community spirit in Falkirk and Stirling for their hospitals'. There would be no immediate change and additional capital expenditure would be allocated to both.

But by then the campaigners, and the Infirmary staff, were facing another battle. Widespread rumours suggested that the special baby care unit opened at a cost of nearly £9 million only three years earlier was going to close and move to Stirling.   There was certainly agreement that having two such units was 'medically and morally unacceptable' and could cost lives because of the dilution of staff and equipment resources. Falkirk received a boost in September when the Stirling Health Council representing medical opinion in the town opted for Falkirk Royal as the best place for a centralised unit because its facilities were much better than the older ones in Stirling which required considerable upgrading. Despite this the unit did eventually move to Stirling as a 'temporary measure' though, as we will see, the whole question of maternity, women's and children's sevices and special baby care would continue to be the subject of much debate in the following years.

Amid all the debate and argument new developments did go ahead at FDRI. In January 1992 a major new facility was opened to provide specialist dentistry, oral surgery, orthodontics and endoscopy at a cost of over £1 million. It was the first of its kind in a district general hospital in Scotland and had the most advanced equipment in the country. While the new suite was under construction a BBC film crew visited the Infirmary as part of a documentary on the use of anaesthetics in dentistry. Along with the new facilities came a new Consultant appointment which meant that patients who had previously had to travel to Glasgow or Edinburgh could be treated nearer home.

If the very survival of FDRI and its specialist facilites preoccupied staff and management throughout the early 1990s it was certainly not the only major talking point. The way in which health care in Forth Valley was managed changed very significantly as the era of 'trusts' emerged from the prevailing political philosophy of the day. Back in 1989 the then Conservative Government in Westminster launched its controversial proposals to allow hospitals to apply for trust status which would mean that they would be governed and managed independently. They would then bid for NHS work from the local Health Board which would remain responsible for securing the appropriate standard of health care in its area. It would still be 'free at the point of delivery' and so the founding principle of the NHS would remain. The argument was that the change would allow closer links with communities and the GP service, and make the providers more responsive to patient needs — the promise of reduced waiting lists and higher throughput of patients was also held out as a benefit. But fears of back-door privatisation were expressed by many both within and outwith the profession and in Forth Valley there appeared to be no appetite for such radical change. However by 1992 the idea was back on the table and in June the Health Board made formal application to the Secretary of State to create a Stirling Royal Infirmary NHS Trust which was approved in April 1993. Of course it was not long before Falkirk Royal followed Stirling with its application and just a year later the Falkirk and District Royal Infirmary Health Service Trust was born.

As part of the preparation for the new arrangements FDRI had adopted a new management structure headed by Mike Kelly as General Manager. Mike had arrived in Falkirk the previous summer from a senior management position with the NHS in Renfrew and it was his responsibility to prepare for the great changeover. Supporting Mike were nine Directors including such well kent faces as Douglas Harper in Surgery, Alistair Barton in Facilities and Margaret Milne in Nursing, Mr Harper had been a member of the surgical team since 1976 and Alistair had also clocked up over 15 years in a variety of positions including taking a leading role in publicity events, fund-raising activities and the recent centenary celebrations. Margaret Milne had returned to FDRI in 1989 to take over from Jean Blackwood and as well as heading up the nursing directorate she was asked to take responsibilty for quality management. The Infirmary too had a new look to greet the changed world. 'New Beginnings' proclaimed the headline of the *Glancet* magazine for June 1993 above an artist's impression of the planned new entrance from Westburn Avenue. This was duly completed towards the end of the year and officially opened by the new Trust's first Chairman, Falkirk pharmacist Ian Mullen who had been a member of the Forth Valley Health Board since 1987. He would go on to chair the succeeding body, NHS Forth Valley, and help mastermind the development of the the £300 million Forth Valley Royal Hospital in the following decade.

Back in 1994 with trust status secured Mike Kelly became the Chief Executive and, along with the Chairman and Board, set about trying to make the new structures work to secure not only the promised

advantages but to win over the doubters of whom there were more than a few. There was help on hand of course. The Scottish Office had no wish to see the trusts fail and so capital was made available to improve existing facilities across Forth Valley and FDRI certainly saw the benefit.

The very issue of the *Glancet* which had reported on those new beginnings said that

> an unprecedented number of building schemes are underway. The Out-patients waiting area has been refurbished and the new Main Entrance /Day Surgery Unit, Psycho-Geriatric Assessment Unit and Psychiatric Admission Unit are due for completion by summer.

In August 1995 local MP Dennis Canavan was on hand to officially open a new Intensive Care area which cost £1.3 million and was said to be 'the most up-to-date, modern facility in the country'. The following summer it was turn of one of the 'Cinderella' services to receive a welcome upgrade. Under the headline 'Grotty Grotto no more' *The Glancet* announced the opening of a new dispensary in the basement pharmacy. With over 4,000 prescriptions dispensed every month —

to out-patients as well as in-patients on discharge, and to external bodies like the Scottish Ambulance Service, Strathcarron Hospice and Polmont YOI — it was obvious that the existing access arrangements were unsatisfactory. Chief Pharmacist Stephen Peddie and his staff of 26, including seven pharmacists, now had a dispensery that people could reach from the main corridor and from a door in the car park, as well as a new waiting area and dispensing counter. In the same year a new stand-alone department of Orthopaedics and Trauma was established at Falkirk Royal with a new team of consultants offering regular clinics covering all the main injuries and conditions. It was another indicator of the demographic changes with which all health providers were having to grapple — the older the patients the more likely they were to need hip and other joint replacements. Interestingly though there was also an upsurge in sports injury cases as the medical teams developed new techniques to keep players on the ball for longer! Finally in 1996, Princess Margaret, sister of Queen Elizabeth, came to the town to open a new in-house nursery, the Beehive, with space for 60 children of staff and the public.

There were also a number of additions to the Infirmary's equipment including a new mammography machine in the X-ray department along with a daylight film processor both designed to improve the service by cutting down on waiting times in what was becoming a very important area of work.

Between 1993 and 1998 the two big infirmaries were, in theory at least, rivals for NHS work and Forth Valley Health Board was able to use its 'buying power' to redistribute services between the two. This led inevitably to tension as specialisms were concentrated in one and reduced in the other. At this stage and for some time afterwards both Trusts seemed determined to retain as comprehensive a range of services as possible and in this they were backed by local, and often very vocal, public opinion. In 1995 for example difficulty in recruiting and retaining paediatric doctors led to calls for a single site at one of the infirmaries. Clinicians strongly supported this proposal which, of course, made perfect sense. The burning question was, which town would lose out? When the Health Board announced that it would move all paediatric services to Stirling as a temporary measure, the balloon went up and Falkirk politicians were again to the forefront.

This time they pressed their arguments with the support of the Falkirk Trust which made a powerful case for retention and in association with the *Falkirk Herald* which mounted yet another campaign under the banner of 'Hands off our Hospital'. Despite this the decision was implemented in July 1995 and the Falkirk Trust's official journal, *The Glancet*, thundered its disapproval 'Paediatrics centralised against the public interest', ... but the deed was done!

Another sign of changing times was the decision in 1996 to close the Forth Valley College of Nursing and Midwifery building at the Infirmary. It had only opened in 1983 but as the demands of the profession changed a permanent link with a University offered real opportunites for staff development. Degree courses were not new but as new drugs and treatments, and high technology equipment, became the norm, more and more members of the nursing staff were expected to undertake complicated medical procedures which demanded a higher level of educational qualification.   Craig Mair sums up the changed situation in his new history of Stirling Royal:

> Before long degree-trained nurses were undertaking many of the tasks previously done by junior doctors, such as taking blood or operating the increasingly sophisticated array of hi-tech equipment now found in hospitals . . . On the other hand, things like taking temperatures or pulses, emptying bed-pans, changing dressings and generally making patients more comfortable, which for a century had been the standard image of nurses, were increasingly undertaken now by a new breed of auxiliary nurses. 'Aye, they can work a CAT machine, which is great, but they cannae make a bed,' joked one retired nurse recently of her modern counterparts.

The College became a Faculty of the University of Stirling and the building at Gartcows was redesignated as the Headquarters of the Falkirk Royal Infirmary NHS Trust.

One of the declared aims of Trust was to make the Infirmary more responsive to patients needs and to see them as customers who ought to be treated well and offered a high quality experience. There was much talk of reducing waiting lists and setting targets for the time taken to see patients after GP referrals. As part of this Falkirk Royal launched a series of 'charters' including A 'Patient's Charter', a 'Children's Charter' and a 'Childbirth Charter' spelling out what patients could expect to receive in Falkirk and District Royal Infirmary. It was a reflection of a new world where public expectations, even demands, were much higher than ever before. A whole host of new procedures some involving highly complex interventions and sophisticated and expensive equipment had been developed and patients everywhere expected that they would be available to them as and when required. It was unrealistic of course but that didn't stop criticism when things were not delivered with the required level of speed and efficiency. Organ transplants, key hole

surgery, MRI scanning, joint replacement, new cancer treatments, new screening techniques all called for higher levels of staff training and much new technology and it was increasingly clear that a provincial hospital like FDRI could not provide everything. Add to that the changing demographic which brought a steady increase in the number of elderly patients requiring specialist geriatric care and looked likely to place huge strains on bed and staff provision in the decades to come.

Despite these increasing demands, the Trust continued to add to the existing facilities as far as budgets would allow. In 1997 Sam Galbraith, Minister of State for Health and the Arts, and a medical man himself, came to open the new 5th Operating Theatre and, as our picture shows, to subject himself to a number of diagnostic tests using some of the new equipment in the Infirmary. And the following year Dennis Canavan was back again to open a new Dermatology Day Care Unit.

Sam Galbraith MP, Minister of State, in the new 5th Theatre

Meantime, the Health Board had to deal with the aftermath of the paediatrics row. Once the dust had settled, the discussion moved on to consider other specialist areas where the same solution — amalgamation on one or other site — seemed to offer the prospect of better care for the population. For the Health Board such rationalisation was essential but with two trusts determined to use their independence to preserve local services there was a real problem. Clearly regular public spats involving the local media and politicians could only lead to ill feeling, falling morale and serious delay and this was in nobody's interest. The Board made the bold decision to merge the Stirling and Falkirk Trusts creating instead a new body, The Forth Valley NHS Acute Hospitals Trust which came into being in 1998. From then on the arguments would be resolved within the committees of the Board and the Trust and presented to the public for discussion and comment. This did not of course stop public debate or argument about new proposals which continued with vigour for the next decade but it did force representatives from both sides to take a more balanced view of what was of best benefit to all the people of the region and not only one corner. As part of this more collegiate approach the future of acute hospital provision could be discussed in a calmer and more constructive atmosphere and this it was hoped would allow progress to be made.

At this stage the vision of the future was still based on two hospitals with centralisation of some specialisms. In August 2000 the Board launched a major three month public consultation around proposals developed by the Trust which included the retention of both Stirling and Falkirk Infirmaries with each offering 'day care investigation and treatment units' known as 'Walk in, Walk out' clinics. Stirling would become a centre for excellence in surgery and Falkirk in women's and children's services including of course maternity. This last proposal was in keeping with the findings of an expert group which had reported a year earlier and had concluded that the Falkirk area had a higher birth rate than Stirling and higher levels of deprivation, a key component in producing complications in childbirth. The consultation involved public meetings and presentations across Falkirk, Stirling and Clackmannan as well as many written submissions and in early 2001 Board members began their consideration of the results. But what emerged from these deliberations did not resolve the major problem. Medical opinion was still strongly in favour of a much more radical solution and there was a growing feeling that the proposals on offer however attractive represented a missed opportunity. It was back to the drawing board.

As the new Millennium dawned Falkirk and District Royal Infirmary was facing unprecedented difficulties yet amazingly the hard pressed medical and support staff coped remarkably well and continued to provide a high level of quality service. Most members of the public still talked with enthusiasm about 'our infirmary' and expressed their admiration for the staff and the care they and their family received. There was sympathy for the problems experienced and complaints, such as they were, tended to focus on administrative matters like shortage of parking spaces or the occasional failure of communication which led to misunderstandings or delays. No doubt many of the staff themselves did not see it quite this way — there were uncertainties about the future, but they coped . . . and hoped for better times to come as the 21st century began. Throughout these difficult times the support groups continued to dig deep to assist in the caring work of the nurses and doctors, a fact underlined by yet another gift, in early 2002, when the faithful WRVS handed over £30,000 part of which was to be used to refurbish the Windsor Unit and part to provide new orthopaedic chairs.

Not long after the completion of the big public consultation there was yet another significant change at the top. In 2001 the Forth Valley Health Board reformed itself as the Forth Valley NHS Board with direct management responsibilites for the Acute Hospitals Trust and the Primary Care Trust, which looked after local health centres etc. In September 2002 Ian Mullen took over as Chairman of the Board and immediately signalled his determination to 'put any previous delay behind us and make firm decisions that will secure services in Forth Valley'. The following year, in February 2003, the Labour Government issued a White Paper called 'Partnership for Care' spelling out its aspirations for a healthier Scotland with services which were even more responsive to patient needs and which offered high quality health care in modern hospitals with shorter waiting times. The existence of 'health inequalities' and what could be done to tackle them became a major concern as were the high levels of heart disease and cancer in Scotland. Almost inevitably one of the Government's recipes for promoting change was yet another restructuring of local management and NHS Boards were directed to dissolve their trusts and replace them with a unified NHS Board. Thus, in March 2004 both trusts were wound up and NHS Forth Valley was born, immediately assuming responsibilty for all heath provision in the areas covered by Falkirk, Stirling and Clackmannan local authorities. Ian Mullen continued to chair the new body working alongside Fiona Mackenzie as Chief Executive. By that time the most significant decision in eighty years of hospital care in Falkirk had already been made and what followed from it is the final part of this story.

CHAPTER NINE

Happy Endings

In early 2003 the long debate on the future of acute hospital provision was drawing to a close with all parties, including most members of the public, ready to accept that a new hospital was necessary, and the sooner the better! What remained to be decided was where it would be located. Beginning in September 2002 the Board had conducted a 96 day formal consultation involving staff, patients and the public and 5,626 people across Forth Valley responded to a number of key questions on the need for a new hospital and its possible location. As expected the overwhelming majority supported the new hospital but almost inevitably there was a split on where it should be. The Board had tentatively suggested the site occupied until 2003 by the Royal Scottish National Hospital (RSNH) at Larbert and this was favoured by the Falkirk respondents and rejected by many of the folk from Stirling. Several alternative suggestions were made of which a site at Pirnhall seemed the most popular. Having digested the results of the survey and held other consultative meetings with the public the Board made their momentous decision in July 2003. The new state-of-the art, multi-million pound hospital would be built at Larbert on the 320 acres of land already owned by NHS Forth Valley and in a beautiful setting that would offer the tranquility of a semi-rural location yet be close to the major centres of population and transport networks. To the people of Falkirk it was good news but disappointed many from Stirling especially in the rural west and north. But to the clinicians it was the red letter day they had hoped for and worked so hard to bring about. The scale of the planned project was staggering. At an estimated cost of £300 million the huge complex would have 860 beds, 16 operating theatres and 4,000 rooms equipped with the most up to date equipment available. The planned floor area was not far short of 100,000 square metres and 70 acres of woodland would be developed

Chairman Ian Mullen unveils the model of the new hospital

to provide therapeutic country walks for both patients, staff and visitors. The project would be funded through a private partnership initiative and built by the contractors Laing O'Rourke headed by Project Leader Lindsay McGibbon, a local man who was born within a stone's throw of the RSNH site.   Once completed the ancillary functions such as maintenance, catering, portering etc. would be managed by SERCO one of the world's leading facilites management companies. It was a very different approach from the past but it was the way in which massive projects were structured in 21st century Britain and NHS Forth Valley accepted it as an inevitable step on its way to providing the Forth Valley population with world class health care facilities. As well as the acute hospital, Falkirk and Stirling would have new Community Hospitals offering a range services similar to the excellent new facility under construction in Clackmannanshire.

Two years later, in May 2006, the plans for the Larbert hospital were unveiled to the public and by March 2007 the site had been cleared of the old RSNH buildings prior to work commencing in May that year. In November the Chairman performed the formal foundation laying ceremony and from then on all eyes were on the Larbert site as a huge team of architects, surveyors, civil engineers, landscape

The site in February 2008

designers and builders, along with
hundreds of tradesmen in every
discipline, set about realising the
dream in bricks and mortar, wood
and glass and lots of shiny metal!

Maureen Coyle was appointed
Project Director by NHS Forth
Valley and for the next three years
her every waking hour was given
over to holding together all the
elements which needed to work in
harmony if the timetable was to be
achieved. So many people, so many
firms, so many stakeholders inside
and outside the NHS, so many

Laying the foundations

things that could go wrong . . . . but thankfully not too many did. It
was the biggest civil engineering project in Scotland at the time
employing 1,500 workers and there was considerable interest at
national level not least from the Scottish Government. Nicola
Sturgeon, Cabinet Secretary for Health and Wellbeing donned the
hardhat and day glow jacket for a site visit in August 2008 and six
months later the First Minister, Alex Salmond performed the topping
out ceremony to signal the completion of the construction phase of
the project. Now it was the turn of the electrical and mechanical
engineers, the joiners, plumbers, plasterers and electricians to finish
the buildings inside and out to the very high specifications determined
by the Board and the architects. On the surrounding land too the
work had proceeded apace with huge carparks with free parking spaces
for 1,500 patients, visitors and staff, and landscaped areas of greenery
designed to enhance the natural beauty of the site. The whole project
moved forward keeping close to the original timetable and elsewhere,
in Stirling and Falkirk, staff and managers prepared for the huge
logistical task which was coming their way.

Commonsense dictated that if services, such as maternity and
accident and emergency, were delivered on two separate sites they
should begin their integration before the move to the new hospital. It
was critically important that the smoothest possible final transfer took

First Minister Alex Salmond 'tops out' the building

place for the wellbeing of patients and staff, and so the inevitable mergers had to take place as soon as possible. No one doubted the logic of this but, of course, questions were asked about where they would be centred for the time being. In the end both big services moved to Stirling and the Falkirk public, for the most part, rested content in the knowledge that in the end they would return with almost everything else to the district. Maternity closed its Falkirk doors in 2004 and A & E moved the following year; how Stirling managed to cope with this huge increase in workload within the physical confines of their deteriorating and overcrowded site is a remarkable part of the story. Some Falkirk folk found travelling to Stirling to visit a major headache especially trying to find a place to park in the vacinity of the Infirmary; and a few Falkirk 'patriots' were disappointed that their offspring were born 'Sons of the Rock' and not 'Falkirk Bairns' but that was about it. Most accepted that all would come right in the end and that meantime they had no choice but to put up with the inconvenience.

The new hospital nears completion

Remarkable as the new hospital project was, there was an even more amazing story unfolding in both existing hosptals. With management time, energy and resources directed for the most part towards Larbert, the medical and support staff in Falkirk and Stirling continued to offer high quality care to the public. Despite the dislocations caused by transfers and the switching of services and equipment, the needs of the patients were always to the fore. Overwhelmingly things went very well and many people had cause to be grateful for the excellent treatment received in Falkirk and Stirling Royal even in the last days before the move to Larbert. With much of the public attention focussed on the new hospital it is right to acknowledge the efforts of the many unsung heroes and heroines who played their part in keeping things functioning and laid the foundation for what was to follow.

It would be wrong however to suggest that the two hospitals were left to 'get on with it' with minimal support from the top. A number of major initiatives occurred at Falkirk Royal during the period between the announcement of the Larbert hospital and the final transfer of patients. For example in April 2006 a new Endoscopy Suite was operational and the next month an MRI Scanning Centre was opened as a collaborative project with the private company Alliance Medical.

The Chairman and Chief Executive with Nicola Sturgeon MSP

It was, said the publicity, 'the selective use of the private sector'. Before this a moble scanner visited Falkirk twice per week and at other times patients requiring immediate scanning had to travel to Glasgow. Now with the new dedicated equipment waiting times which had been 18 weeks in 2004 fell to a remarkable 2 weeks in 2006. The following year on 3rd September Nicola Sturgeon was again in Falkirk, this time to open a £600,000 renal dialysis unit which increased the number of patients who could be treated from 68 per week to 100. The new technology was impressive with each patient issued with a chip and pin swipe card containing all their dialysis and prescription needs. But it was not all high technology in the new NHS world. All across the country new staff uniforms appeared and they could scarcely be any more different than the starchy style beloved of traditionalists. They were it was claimed more comfortable to wear, helped identify the roles of the staff and would save the NHS thousands of pounds through bulk purchasing. Trousers replaced skirts and various shades of green and blue identified clinical, domestic, catering and other support staff. The picture on the next page cannot of course capture the colour code but at least it shows the new style! They would soon be seen everywhere in the new hospital which by then was well underway.

The new uniforms: navy blue in the middle for senior charge nurses

Following the completion of the physical structure the project team set about installing the furniture and equipment. Again the statistics are staggering. Over 150,000 separate items, nearly 60% coming from the two infirmaries and the rest completely new, had to be packed up, moved to Larbert and made to work in their new location with minimal delay. As well as the MRI scanner and two CT scanners there were 16 anaesthetic machines, 10 dental surgeries, 7 digital general X-ray rooms, 171 electric examination couches, 1396 clocks and thousands of other essential items ... not forgetting the high tech equipment of Radio Royal due for installation high above the atrium on the very RSNH site where they had first broadcast back in 1977. By the summer of 2010 the first phase of the project was judged complete and the operation to move patients from Falkirk began. Medical and surgical wards, day surgery, renal dialysis, chemotherapy, operating theatres, X-ray, dental and endoscopy services were the first to arrive followed in September by the transfer of acute inpatient mental health services from Falkirk and Stirling. The guarantee offered to patients and visitors was unlike anything most had experienced before:

> If you're an in-patient you'll be cared for in either a single room
> with en suite facilities or a spacious four bedded ward. You'll also
> have access to a free personal TV and enjoy hospital meals which
> are freshly prepared on site each day . . . . The new hospital has a
> wide range of facilities to make your stay or visit as pleasant and
> comfortable as possible including a restaurant, Starbucks coffee
> shop, W H Smith and a WRVS cafe.

In other words the kind of facilities on offer in a quality hotel but
coupled with the best medical treatment available. And there were
other innovations like separate patient corridors, lifts offering greater
privacy and, most amazing of all, a team of 'robots' transporting bed
linen, meal trolleys, clinical waste and medical supplies throughout
the building in their own private corridors. The pharmacy has its own
robotic system with clever machines capable of labelling medicines,
stacking shelves, picking up prescriptions and delivering drugs to the
wards. Inevitably these space-age assistants, the first of their kind in
a UK hospital, attracted a great deal of publicity in those first days as
the media both press, radio and television brought news of Forth Valley
Royal Hospital to the nation. The 'Royal' title had been confirmed by

A special edition of Forth Valley News in September 2010 announces the completion of the Hospital and the start of the patient transfer. It contained messages of goodwill from local civic leaders and praise from the public for all those who had pooled their talents to create such a fantastic facility.

Buckingham Palace in January 2010 as a fitting honour for the successor to two Royal Hospitals, Stirling given the name back in 1874 by Queen Victoria, and Falkirk similarly honoured in 1932 by King George V. And, of course, the Royal connection did not end there. In 1928 King George VI and Queen Elizabeth (then the Duke and Duchess of York) had opened the new Stirling Infirmary building at Livilands and four years later, Prince George, younger brother of the Duke, had done the same for the new Falkirk Infirmary at Gartcows. As plans were made for the official opening at Larbert there were high hopes for something similar and to the delight of local people the Board was able to announce that Her Majesty Queen Elizabeth and the Duke of Edinburgh would came to Larbert on 6th July 2011. On the big day the heavens opened but the foul weather did not deter either the Royal party or the staff and guests who turned out in large numbers for what was a memorable occasion and a fitting climax to the years of planning and construction. While the Queen visited the oncology and physiotherapy departments with Chairman Ian Mullen, Prince Philip accompanied by Chief Executive Fiona Mackenzie, met up with the famous robots before returning to the atrium for the formalities which included unveiling a plaque and signing the visitors' book. But for

most people present the high point was the magic moment when three year old Hayley Boyle, granddaughter of the Lord Lieutenant Marjory McLachlan, decided that since another little girl had just presented the Queen with a posy of flowers she should add her own greeting in the form of an impromptu hug! 'Squeezed to meet you, your Highness' was the *Scotsman*'s next day headline as the image of an unihibited little child became, for a moment, the symbol of a happy and successful day.

With the formalities over the project team moved on to the final phase of the transfer from Stirling of, among others, the Maternity and Accident and Emergency Departments. All went according to plan and by the end of July the new Hospital was fully operational though it would be sometime before all the loose ends were fully tied up. The hospital had been delivered on schedule and on budget and those responsible might have been forgiven if they had decided to sit back and relax in the aftermath of their successful endeavours. But there was much more still to do. As the transfers proceeded thoughts had turned once again to the services which would remain in the new Falkirk Community Hospital. It had always been part of the overall plan that each community, in Falkirk, Stirling and Clackmannan, would have its own centre providing basic hospital services. When Ian Mullen made public the decision to build new at Larbert he had prefaced his remarks by saying:

> We believe that where possible, patients should be treated closer to home in community hospitals and health centres. When they do have to come to hospital, services should be focussed on their needs and provided in purpose built facilites.

After the major relocation from Falkirk to Larbert the 'Falkirk Community Hospital' signs went up and the staff who remained continued to provide a wide range of local services. The plan was that rehabilitation, palliative care, community dental services, speech and language therapy, dietetics, sexual health and psycholgy would continue to be provided in either a new built facility or in some of the existing buildings which could be adapted for the purpose. Plans were also made to review the future location of adult mental health facilities presently located at Westbank and Dunrowan. Much depended on the availability of finance but unfortunately the international crisis which emerged in 2008 brought funding reductions across the whole of the public service. Plans required to be modified and the prospect of new buildings receded for the time being. At the time of writing a number of buildings on the huge Gartcows site are being demolished — the 1987 Maternity and Windsor Units have already gone — and the fate of the iconic front building with the clock, name and royal coat-of-arms is uncertain. Many hope it can be saved and put to use for the community as a reminder to future generations of the fund-raising campaign of the 1920s, the greatest communal effort in the history of the district.

Talk of fund-raising brings to mind the long standing contribution of the Friends of Falkirk and District Royal Infirmary mentioned several times already in this story. Now in 2011 they decided that since FDRI was no more they would change their name to the Friends of Forth Valley Royal Hospital. In May they held a special evening to mark the change when former Matron Agnes Cadger and founder member of the Friends back in 1957, Jean Caldwell, cut special cakes. From now on, under the leadership of Chairman Bob Ness and Secretary Sandra Peat, the Friends will support both the Forth Valley Royal and Falkirk Community Hospital.

But final decisions on what will survive and what will go where in the Community Hospital are for the future. Today is a time for celebration as the people of Falkirk and district embrace the new Forth Valley Royal Hospital, the very worthy successor of the Thornhill Road and Gartcows buildings which meant so much to people past and present. Goodness knows what dear old Mrs Gibson in 1889, or Matron Anna Dick and her team of nurses in 1932, would have made of

The Friends celebrate in May 2011: Sandra Peat, Pat Stanners, Alison Harris, Agnes Cadger, Bob Ness, Jean Caldwell, Ian Mullen and Elspeth Thomson

the amazing facilities at Larbert. Utter astonishment and disbelief no doubt — even those born in the space age find the scale and complexity of today's provision almost beyond imagination. And yet, as this history has shown, the reality is that from 1889 until 2011 the guiding principle has been the same. It is a simple mission. To care for the sick and injured to the very best of our ability and, if humanly possible, to return them to their homes and families healed and restored. There is surely no greater calling than this. The Good Samaritan whose image has been a powerful symbol throughout the life of Falkirk and District Royal Infirmary, along with the motto of both town and infirmary, 'Touch ane, touch a', remain as a reminder of that guiding principle and of 120 years of faithful service which continues today and will surely do so for all the generations to come.

Index